An Island Christmas

Nollaig Oileánach

An Island Christmas

Nollaig Oileánach

Micheál Ó Conghaile

Translated from Irish by

Mícheál Ó hAodha

MERCIER PRESS

Mercier Press

www.mercierpress.ie

First published in Irish as *Nollaig Oileánach* by Cló Iar-Chonnacht, An Spidéal, Co. na Gaillimhe in 2022.

This edition in English published by Mercier Press in 2023.

ISBN: 978-1-78117-846-1

978-1-78117-847-8 eBook

Printed and bound in the EU.

Contents

In memory of
Máirtín Ó Direáin, 1910–1988

I

THIS, OUR ISLAND

———◆———

I'm going to describe an island Christmas to you and I'll be as accurate and concise as possible in my depiction. And even if I'm a bit slow in the telling at times, have patience with me please. It's only that I'm trying to bring memories to mind again, slowly and naturally, recalling them in their own natural shape and form from my life fifty years ago. And you might pause briefly with me for a short while every now and then too …

Inis Treabhair (Inishtravin) is the name of the island I'm from originally. But where will I begin with my story? With the name of the place itself perhaps, and the fact that the island was often called by another name too: Inis Trá Mhóir, as once used in the school roll book – because of the big strands that surround the island, the extensive shorelines on every side. Many's the time we walked the length of them in our black and green wellingtons. Or in our shoes sometimes. If we were caught out by the tide, we'd try and stand up on the higher flagstones and the rocks so that our feet weren't drowned wet and sank into the mire. The mire is the mud that you find on many of the shores here and it's grey and very soft. But we'll leave the grey mud and the boggy ground aside for a moment. We won't bother with it too much in this account even if it was never too far away from us back then, whenever we were out on the strand picking periwinkles or gathering limpets and seaweed on the many shorelines around Inis Trá Mhóir or Inis Treabhair.

As for the island itself, it's a very small island, about a mile long, that's all. It takes about a quarter of an hour of quick walking to go from the eastern end of the island to the west, from An Caladh ó Dheas (South Harbour) or An Caladh Thuaidh (North Harbour) back to An Caladh Mór (Big Harbour) that's at the furthest western tip of the island completely. The island is shaped in a figure of eight as laid on its side, a fact that means it forms two halves almost right at its centre. This is very obvious when it's at full tide as all that's left in the middle of it is an area of about fifty metres or so. There's another harbour there known as Caladh na Sliogán (Shell Harbour) and a quay called An Chéibh Nua (The New Quay), although the latter saw very little use during my time on the island; no one lived on the western half of the island back then. The island itself is located in the area known as Ceantar na nOileán, west of Eanach Mheáin (Annaghvaan) and it was out to Eanach Mheáin Quay mainly that the Inis Treabhair islanders travelled in their timber currachs when I was young to go shopping or undertake any other business on the mainland. South of Inis Treabhair you have Cuan Bhrandaí (Brandy Harbour), an Doirín Glas, Cnoc Leitir Móir (Lettermore Hill) and Cnoc Leitir Calaidh (Lettercallow Hill). North of the island, you have Ros Muc (Rosmuc) and Ros Cíde (Roskeeda) and back west of them again is Coill Sáile (Kylesalia). Situated directly west of the Inis Treabhair stands Cill Chiaráin (Kilkieran), looking out across the bay. I mentioned an interesting and unusual place name just now Cuan Bhrandaí or Brandy Harbour in English, a place that got its name from the brandy that was smuggled ashore there from Spain and France a few hundred years ago, according to tradition.

Now you know where Inis Treabhair is in case you ever want to strike out for there and visit it someday in the future. What would bring you there in the first place? I'm not sure myself to be honest. You might visit out of curiosity maybe? People are always curious. Or you might visit the island out of a sense of adventure or if you wished to make a trip to somewhere that is a bit different. I know one thing that won't attract visitors there and that's the social life, because no one at all lives on the island anymore!

The last person to live there was Pádraig Ó Loideáin, or Patsy Lydon as we knew him. He left the island in

2010 and no one has lived there on a continuous basis ever since, even if some of the island's descendants and their families go in and out to Inis Treabhair regularly because they still have cattle and lands there. Máire and Frank Ó Faogáin from Ráth Chairn, whose people came from the island originally, have done up the old schoolhouse and spend time there every now and then; other than the Ó Faogáin's, the island is uninhabited for most of the year however. Consequently, if you visit the island someday, you may find yourself alone there except for the company of the noisy, shrieking gulls and crows and all the different insects and animals that make their home there.

And were there many people living on the island back when you were a child, you ask? Just a few people to be honest. Very few. Inis Treabhair's era was already coming to an end even when I was a child. People were already leaving for the mainland or emigrating abroad even then, their houses left empty and abandoned. Decades earlier, just before the Great Famine, about 100 people lived on the island, nearly twenty families or so in total. After the Famine, in the 1870s, the population increased to more than 150 people or twenty-two families altogether. My father, Coilmín Tom Veail was born in 1917 and he remembered around fifteen houses or so that were still inhabited when he was young. By the time I was growing up in the 1960s however, there were just five or six houses that were occupied; less than forty people altogether, between young and old; it was a tiny population.

The Réamainn family and Nóra Uí Mhullaoidh lived down by the Caladh ó Dheas (South Pier). We always referred to them as 'na Réamainn' in Irish and there were eleven children in the family, all of them in and around the same age as ourselves. Two members of the family died recently, Pádraic, the eldest in the family and Gearóid, who was the youngest God rest them both. Gearóid was the youngest person left who was born and reared on the island. We lived a quarter of a mile back the road from them.

There were eight of us in it, and, in addition to my parents, an uncle of ours, Pádraic Tom Veail, lived in our house too. 'Na Veaileanna' is what we were called on the island with reference to my great-grandfather. But strangely enough, and for some reason that I don't understand, we were known as 'na Coilmíní' over on the mainland, where we were named after my father. But we were all the one crowd really, and everyone on the island knew this, even if a system like this could sometimes confuse a stranger or an outsider to the area.

Across the fields from us, and we could see their house from the road, was the Catháin's house. There were ten in that family but most of them had already emigrated to England when I was a boy. I only knew the three

11

youngest children who were still at home then, as well as their mother Ellen. Their father, Darachín Chatháin, died a long time before I was born. I did get to know many of the others in the family, the ones who'd left Ireland, in the summer of 1971 when their eldest son Cóilín was killed in a bad accident over in England. His body was brought home to Ireland after a few weeks and most of the family came back to Inis Treabhair and spent some time back in the home place that summer.

Over east at An Caladh ó Thuaidh is where the two Sonaí's' lived. Colm Ó Nia or Sonaí Chóilín Choilm and his wife Mary Neidín Sweeney from Leitir Calaidh. Sonaí Chóilín was the oldest person living on the island and they had no children. Across the wall from them – the two houses were very close to one another – lived Sonaí Mhicil Mharcaisín Ó Conghaile and his wife Mary. There were seven children in that family but the older ones had emigrated to America when I was a child, which meant that I didn't know them very well at the time. One of them, Cóilín, died in America recently, may he rest in peace; his ashes were later brought home and scattered on the island.

An unusual thing about the two Sonaí's – or something that seemed unusual to me as a child anyway – was that they each kept a gun in their house. The guns were hung from special pins or hooks above the hearth even if they were rarely used as far as I could tell. They used them to shoot birds the odd time, that's all I remember. Sonaí Chóilín used his gun to shoot the odd cormorant, even if I'm not sure how good a shot he had. As it happens, both Sonaí's could have been members of the Old-IRA and this is how they'd had the guns. But I could be mistaken about this too. Sonaí Chóilín was certainly in the Old-IRA anyway, I know this for certain. He'd even trained and drilled with Patrick Pearse when the latter was based in Ros Muc, just across the sea from us. As for the other Sonaí – Sonaí Mhicil Mharcaisín – as he was known – his baptismal name was Micheál. One of his sons was also called Micheál as this was a custom that was very strong on the island and throughout Connemara generally – i.e. that the father's name and the mother's name also – would be given to one of the sons and one of the daughters. It wasn't a tradition that I was that fond of myself, even if I'm not sure why. Given that there were three Micheál Ó Conghaile's on the island at the same time it meant that the postman got confused sometimes and the letters were mixed up the odd time. Not that it ever caused any trouble between us – only that it could be a bit awkward at times. To tell you the truth, the island people didn't receive that many letters at the time anyway. Still, I've often said to myself since then – that even if I had a thousand sons myself, I'd never call any of them Micheál – not even if I was running out of names! But there's little chance of that happening. I'd put 'Colm' after my surname to differentiate between us.

So there you go now with a small bit of background on every family that lived on Inis Treabhair when I lived there. Well – almost anyway. Because two other families lived there also when I was around, one family that left and one that returned to the island. On an incline, above An Chaladh ó Thuaidh lived the family of the Tomás Dharach Ó Mullaoidh, a first cousin of Réamonn Ó Mullaoidh. There were eight children in the family but Tomás died young in August 1966 when I was just four. I can just about remember him still. Strangely enough, the image I have of him is one where he comes back as if in a dream and walks around alone through the island fields; and he is weeping because he has already died. I didn't have much understanding of death at that age, it goes without saying. Many long years later, a range of characters would come back from the dead in my own fiction writing as if as a natural aspect of the stories; whether this has any connection with the childhood memories or not, I'm not sure. I still remember Tomás' wife Peige and how she'd always give us big handfuls of raisins as a treat anytime we called to their house. There weren't many sweets around at the time anyway but it was even more difficult to get sweets out to an island without a shop in the middle of the sea. Darach's family moved to Leitir Calaidh on the mainland soon after this; the house was closed up and it has been sealed ever since.

The Loideáin family, or two of this family to be exact, returned to live on Inis Treabhair. Their house was right in the middle of the eastern end of the island and located on the most elevated spot there. One of the sons Patsy returned from America and his mother who'd been living with her daughter Mary in Doire Iorrais, Ros Muc, also moved back to the island. The doors and windows of the house were opened again, and fresh air was let into the house and onto the hearth once more. It was in our house that they lodged initially for a few weeks while their own house was being made liveable again. I have fond memories of Nóirín sitting next to the hearth and smoking her pipe sometimes. I remember too her very long grey hair, and how she'd spend a good while combing it out every morning, so that it was always so perfect and neat.

There must've been an old link or friendship going back years between ourselves and the Ó Loideáin's because it was in their house that my grandmother Mary Breathnach died suddenly at a young age from a heart attack on 4 October, 1941; she was just fifty-seven years of age. This was more than twenty years before I was born so obviously I have no memory of her, other than a photo that we had in the sitting room of our house for years.

The chances are that we wouldn't have had that picture of her at all either if she hadn't spent some years in America when she was young because the photo was taken over there. She'd subsequently returned to Ireland, something that was very unusual at the time. My grandmother collapsed and died in the Ó Loideáin's house, right in the middle of the day, when she was over on a visit or passing on a message. The Ó Loideáin's was also the main house in the village that people called to and socialised when I was young. It was a great place for a chat and storytelling and sometimes, the odd piece of music was played there as well. People gathered to play cards in their house, games that went on late into the winter night.

Yes indeed. On a small island, like Inis Treabhair, the options for socialising or having a bit of company were naturally very limited. Everyone lived very close to one another, and of course, we all knew each other well for years anyway. Maybe we knew too much about each other sometimes, but that's another story! And yet, I'd imagine that an island as small as Inis Treabhair was there unknown to most of the world at the time, as with other small islands off the coast of Galway.

When I was thirteen and attending boarding school in Galway city and when I told others that I was from an island off the coast, people immediately assumed that I was from one of the Aran Islands. This used to irritate me as there are – or there were then anyway – many other islands off the Galway coast that people still lived on into the 1960s, and into the 1970s, and even later although they are nearly all abandoned now – Inis Bearachain, Inis an Ghainimh, an tOileán Mór, Daighinis, Inis Éirc or Fínis. But it was always the Aran Islands that I was associated with given that most people had never heard of Inis Treabhair or any of the other small islands off the Galway coast either. Inis Treabhsúr (Trousers Island) some lads would call the island just to tease me! Even if you couldn't make any comparison at all between Inis Mór, Inis Meáin or Inis Oírr and an island such as Inis Treabhair, other than that they were surrounded by the sea. There were nearly 1,000 people living in Inis Mór at the time, about 300 people living on Inis Meáin, and nearly the same again on Inis Oírr. And less than forty people living on Inis Treabhair! You couldn't compare them at all – simple as that! There was nothing really on Inis Treabhair at the time, no shop or church, no lodgings or hotel. None of the houses on the island had electricity or running water when I was young either.

What did we do without a toilet or running water you might ask? Well, I'll tell you straight out. We went out every morning and did our business under a ditch or a bush in some sheltered place. A handful of dock leaves or a few tufts of grass were what you used for toilet paper or some pages torn one of the old newspapers that you brought with you on your way out just to be on the safe side. We drew our own water from the well to have a bath and to wash some part of ourselves anyway. In summertime, all of this was far easier because we could go for a swim in the sea. We loved swimming and it was a chance to revive ourselves and cool down after a long hot day's work outdoors. Many's the summer day, I remember my mother telling us to have a wash when we got home after a long day sweating and working with turf, seaweed, and out in the fields. But I suppose every child at the time was the same as us to be honest, and it didn't bother us much. Yes indeed. Life was far simpler back then in many ways. We mightn't have been as clean-scrubbed and tidy as the children nowadays but we were healthy and strong and could fight off plenty of infections and viruses naturally. I don't remember any of the eight of us having to go to the doctor because we were sick at any stage – not even once when I was young and living on the island! I remember the doctor calling to the island once or twice all right when my father got sick with the mumps that one of my brothers had picked up in boarding school, in St Mary's College, Galway. All of us picked up the mumps at the time if I remember rightly.

When I was seven, my father built a small timber lavatory outside the house that we could use as a toilet, something that made life far easier for us, even if you had to wait your turn sometimes. At night, we kept a pot under every bed and unless you emptied it and scrubbed it clean every morning, there'd be a strong smell from it. 'Ar chaith tú amach an pota?' ('Did you throw out the pot?') was a regular refrain, even if it wasn't the pot itself that was thrown out but its contents instead. Some water to wash it out with and you'd put it back in place again for the following night. 'Mar nach é lá na gaoithe lá na scolb!' or 'Prevention is better than cure!'

Things improved further for us when I was about ten or eleven as my father added a back kitchen to the house as well as a toilet and a bathroom with a water tank above it, so that we had regular water supply. You just pumped the water every day with a hand pump attached to this big tank outside the house. Every drop of rain that fell onto the roof of the house was collected in this big tank, and filtered through the system. It was hard enough work pumping the water daily but it meant that we had running water for the toilet and plenty of water to wash ourselves with, except for the odd summer when you had to be sparing with it if there was a drought for a few weeks. But for the first time we had a proper toilet and bathroom.

Although we had plenty of water in the big tank, we didn't use this to drink or to make tea with; instead, we drank water from Tobar Choilmín (Little Colm's Well), a freshwater well on the eastern side of the island, a well from which everyone on the island drew water from in buckets. This is a beautiful well and the water there was always very healthy and pure. The well was cleaned once or twice a year and was named after Coilmín Ó Loideáin, Patsy Ó Loideáin's grandfather. It was a well that never failed the people of the island, and even when we had very fine summers and a long spell of drought, it never dried up completely. There was always a little drop of water left down at the bottom of it even if you'd to bring a small mug or saucer to dip into it, something which we and the other families on the island did the odd hot dry summer. It is still a fine well even if people rarely draw water from it nowadays.

Most of the food that we ate back then was food we grew for ourselves also. Potatoes and vegetables of all types – cabbage, lettuce, onions, scallions, carrots and parsnips. Large turnips and mangles for the cattle. The seed was set in the spring and the crops harvested in summer and in autumn mainly. We kept chickens and ducks also that we reared and killed for food as well as sheep, goats and a pig that we fattened each year for slaughter. We ate fish also even if we didn't eat that much of it, strangely enough. Salted fish was common even if we didn't do the salting ourselves. I think it was from Aran that my father got the fish, pollock and wrasse mainly. They could last a year or more if properly salted and were very tasty. They'd be left there in a bag or box until they were needed for cooking. This fish tasted very sharp and bitter however, even after being boiled in water a few times to try and take some of the saltiness out of it. As children, it wasn't our favourite dinner of all, but it's worth remembering that we didn't have a huge choice of food at the time either.

As I mentioned earlier there was no electricity on the island! There were no fridges on the island then, never mind electric light, so it was difficult to keep anything fresh for very long, meat and fish especially. Once meat was brought home from the shop, you made sure to eat it within a day or two, in case it went off. Or if you boiled the meat, you might get an extra day or two out of it. We often kept a few cans of tinned meat in storage also in case we had a visitor to the house that we weren't expecting. We also kept cans of peas and beans as well as boxes of dried peas that you soaked in water overnight before eating. I don't remember us having to buy any fresh vegetables at any stage: usually, we grew enough of our own to do us. We rarely bought potatoes other than for a month or two in early-summer before the new potatoes had grown enough to dig them. We bought seed potatoes of course. And the seed potatoes weren't all planted intact in the soil either; they were sliced into pieces first. 'Na sciolláin' is the part of the potato with the eye was called and 'Na baslóga' (potato sprouts) in Irish. The part of the potato that was left over were called 'Na logáin' (pits/small hollows) and these parts of the potato were cooked and eaten.

In addition to working on the island, in the fields and on the shore, there was a fair bit of work and struggle relating to cutting turf and bringing it home. There was no turf cut on the island when I lived there, but the generations before me did harvest turf on Inis Treabhair. There is a stretch of land on the western side of the island called An Portach Mór (The Large Bog), where the people who came before us cut turf for themselves. When I lived there however, most of the turf was bought from people on the mainland and brought over to the island later. As it happens, our family had our own strip of bog on the mainland so that we cut, footed and dried our own turf there. This bog was in Fionnán (Finnaun), which was almost twenty miles from where we lived. Not that this long journey ever bothered us as children because we were lucky enough to have a van; and it was a day out for us on the mainland instead of being stuck at home working at hay or pulling weeds and dock-leaves from the vegetable gardens, and the like. Another big positive about going to the bog was that my father always stopped in Tigh Phíotair or Tigh Kitt, a bar in Doire an Fhéich (Derrynea) on our way home for a few drinks, as did many others returning from working on the bog. He'd always give us money to buy ice cream, sweets and cidona and we'd go into Kitt's shop there or across the road to John Tooles. We were cousins to the Tooles and my father often stopped there do some shopping.

Only island people can understand the difficulty and hardship involved in transporting and bringing supplies onto an island. Normal, everyday, items are difficult enough to transport to an offshore island at the best of times but imagine a lorry-full of turf for instance. I'd be teasing my neighbours sometimes here in Indreabhán (Inverin) and telling them that they have no idea of the hardship and drudgery that working with turf involves really – not when they've a lorry or a tractor and trailer to bring their turf home and to tip it at the gable-end of the house for them. As easy and simple as that!

It was a different story altogether for us when we were bringing the turf home. Firstly, we had to cut the turf with the 'sleán' (slane/turf-spade) of course, then let it dry. We'd foot and re-foot the turf and once it was dried out, the real work began. Given the different methods of transportation involved, it made best sense to gather the turf into bags once it was ready to be brought home. Initially, we used big, sturdy bags for this job, bags that we reused from one year to the next. But then my father got much lighter bags that were easier for the job, Odlums bags, that had been used for flour at one time. My father must've known some baker in Galway city because he got a big load of these bags one day and we used them for many years afterwards. These bags weren't as big as the ones we'd had previously but they were lighter and better for the work.

We used to fill the bags with turf, with one person holding the bag open and one or two others filling it with sods. You filled these bags right up to the top. My father put two or three stitches in each bag with a big three-inch needle he had for such purpose to make sure no sods fell out on our subsequent journey. Then we moved the bags in timber wheelbarrows across the bog and out onto the road, a walk that was anything between fifty and two hundred yards depending on how far back on the bog the turf was cut. A fairly-strong young lad could carry two bags on a wheelbarrow but you had to have your wits about you and plough as firm and steady a course for yourself to steer the wheelbarrow across the bog; otherwise the wheels on the barrow sank into the bog, especially in wet weather. You made sure to avoid any small mounds of heather along the way too, as they could tip your barrow over and made your path out of the bog more difficult and winding again. We loaded the bags into the van then, about sixty of them altogether.

Next came the drive from Fionnán to Eanach Mheáin where we unloaded the bags from the van onto the quayside there. The following day the engine-boat was brought out, all the bags were loaded aboard, and we travelled out to An Chalaidh ó Dheas. Our engine boat was a púcán with an engine installed in it as it was common and more reliable at the time to replace the sails with engines. You had to be strong to throw these bags out onto the pier-side there, a job that was easier when the tide was high. We often followed the tides on this. Normally, two people worked together unloading the turf after which you went out for the donkey and yoked it to the cart. The last bit of the journey involved transporting the bags of turf from the pier-side back to your house, a journey of around a quarter of a mile by road. A cartload comprised about fifteen bags of turf each turn so that there were four or five journeys involved altogether. Back home you untied the bags and built up your reek of turf.

There was a lot more pulling and dragging involved with this than just tipping your turf at the gable end of the house, as was the case on the mainland! We brought about five or six van-loads of turf home to our house on the island like this every year, I'd say. That was a lorry-load and a half of turf each year altogether and it was hard-earned given the extra work involved for island people such as ourselves as compared with the people living on the mainland. Not that we paid that much attention to such work as children really. It was just a normal and familiar aspect of our lives that we enjoyed for the most part, a type of work that we undertook with enthusiasm and energy; we didn't know any different at the time.

Working on the bog over in Fionnán, I remember my father telling us that if we walked in a straight line from the turf-banks in the direction of sea and shore, we'd come out eventually close to the place where the Poitín Stil is today – a place that wasn't that far away from us really -as the crow flies. Now that I live close to the Poitín Stil today myself, I'm often tempted to walk in the opposite direction from the road across the bog to see if I could find those old turf-banks in Fionnán again where I worked and sweated hard as a lad. Yes, indeed – those were the days – as they say!

But, not to worry, I'll finish up now with this discussion of bog-work in days gone by in case it appears too long drawn-out. It's Christmas-time that I wanted to tell the story in this book about, and an Island Christmas in particular for the most part. It's just that I felt it important to provide some background initially, a brief portrait of our working lives back then and how much island life differed to life on the mainland in those days; and, needless to say – as compared with life in the present-day.

Another aspect of our lives that is worth recalling at this point relates to living conditions on the island, and the houses that we lived in. The house I grew in was built at the end of the 1930s by a man from Ros Muc by the name of Sonaí Mór Ó Nia. Our family's old house was on the same site and the new house was built around the old one. The older people stayed living in the old house as long as they could while the new house was being built and went to a neighbouring house for their meals. One day a grand-uncle of mine by the name of Darach arrived home early to the house after dinner to find a girl eating potatoes from a basket in the middle of the floor, except this being that he saw wasn't an earthly creature at all! That was one story anyway! Another story I heard was that the stones from the old house were placed in the walls of the new house. I'd hear my uncle saying that they had a milk cow at the time and she never stopped lowing and bellowing all the while that the old house was being knocked down as much as to say that she was lamenting the old place or that she was afraid that the people of the house might be left homeless. As the wise person once said, the majority of people lived off stories back then, and they still live off them to this very day!

There were two bedrooms in the lower half of the new house, one of which we referred to as 'An Chailleach' (the Hag/the Witch). There were very few houses at the time that didn't have a room known as 'An Chailleach'. This word 'cailleach' and 'elderly woman' are synonymous of course and at the time it was common for a grandmother or grandfather to live with the rest of the extended family.

I suppose you could say that the room known as 'An Chailleach' was the equivalent of what is called a 'granny flat' nowadays. There was a large kitchen in the house. It had an open fire with a hob on either side of it before we installed a range there. We had a big sitting room with a fireplace even though we rarely used it until we got a bit older and the family grew bigger. This sitting room was for visitors mainly, not that we ever had many visitors on the island at the time. To the side of the house, at the rear, away from the sun, was a tiny room known as the 'dairy' and it was here that we stored the milk and butter, in addition to the flour my mother used for kneading and baking. There was also an extra bedroom up on the loft and a ladder leading up to it.

The house didn't have any stairs initially but one was installed after my father married, as well as a loft that included two additional rooms. These two rooms had flagstone windows from which you could see out, far and near. And as mentioned earlier, the comfort of the family was added to when a back kitchen, a toilet and a bathroom were added to the house. Yes indeed, it was in this remote house on an island out in the middle of the ocean, that I spent all of my childhood Christmases.

2

PREPARING FOR CHRISTMAS

As you'd expect, there were many preparations made for Christmas each year. The way I remember it however, we didn't do a whole lot with the house as regards cleaning and painting. It was in summer time or when 'the stations' took place that people really did up their houses. The stations were held on the island twice a year and whatever house it was held in was scrubbed from top to bottom, or at least that part of the house the people of the island gathered. Each house held the stations one after another, a fact which meant that we had the stations in our house every three years or so. Whenever it came around, we cleaned the house from top to bottom and painted all the walls, doors and windows. There was no such thing as PVC windows back then, and it was a right torment painting the windows at the time. Between inside and outside the house, there were so many timbers and sides to each window that it was nearly impossible not to miss some small section of timber, despite your best efforts –

some small section that made a fool of the rest of your work, once the mistake was noticed a day or two later. The exterior walls of the house were whitewashed every summer and this meant that they always had a nice bright, chalk-white sheen to them. The road outside was made neat also by applying sand or daub clay to it. There were a couple of daub holes on the island and you'd shovel it out and clear the stones, big and small from it with a pick, then bring the yellowish daub home in bags on the donkey's back or in a hand-barrow or wheelbarrow after which you spread it out on the road. It smoothed out the surface of the road for a while anyway.

We cleaned the chimney every year, usually before Christmas. Sometimes we cleaned it ourselves but the neighbours often gave us a helping hand with it too, when we were very young. Sometimes during the year, people from outside the Gaeltacht would go from house to house on the island cleaning chimneys and the like. This was the time before ranges became more common and there was an open fire in most houses. Chimneys were often cleaned with a rough brush made from a cluster of bushes and branches bound tightly together. A big bundle of them tied with a rope which were then pulled up and down through the chimney. One person would be up next to the chimney-pot on top of the house and someone else down below at the hearth, and they pulled up and down against one another as hard as they could to clean out as much soot as possible. The soot often ended up all over the floor and the people below often took the brunt of it, especially whoever was closest to the hearth. But this did the job until the brushes with the long extensions became more common, brushes that were specially-made for the task.

As regards the major cleaning that we did every summer there was a lot of work involved with it. Every room in the house had to be done, one after another; all the bedclothes washed and hung out on the line to dry. Every nook and cranny in the house was cleaned from top to bottom and all the walls were painted; even the pictures on the walls had to be taken down and their frames painted. The picture-frames were painted bright-silver or gold usually. There were small special pots of paint available for this task in certain shops in Galway city. The legs and the frames of each table and chair were carefully washed, and the concrete floor of the kitchen was scoured and scrubbed clean as well.

One memory in particular that I have of the stations relates to the 'priest's sugar'. There were very few sweet things available other than sugar when I was a child and everyone, whether young or old, tended to add a couple of spoons of sugar into their mug of tea. They used regular sugar from the bag of course but once the stations came around, sugar cubes had to be got in especially for the priest's breakfast, as we called it – the tea the priest drank after he'd said the station mass. This was why the sugar cubes were commonly referred to as 'the priest's sugar'. You couldn't buy them in many shops in Connemara at the time, I think, so you had to go into Galway to get them so they were on the table the day of the stations. You had to show a great deal of respect to the priests back then, far too much really. Brown sugar was often provided also for the occasion in case the priest preferred this, even if this was another item that people didn't often have themselves, at home.

We reared a pig every year that we slaughtered just before Christmas. My father butchered it – to be more exact. I'm sure that everyone has heard that phrase 'muc i mála' ('pig in a bag' or 'pig in a blanket') and once a year, in spring, my father would come home with a bag inside which something was squealing loudly. It was a banbh (piglet) that we'd feed up and fatten for the rest of the year until it'd grown into a fine, well-fed pig come Christmas-time. We fed the pig mainly on whatever food was left over. The slops of tea and milk left in the teapot or the mugs or crusts of bread with a few potatoes mixed in. Potato skins and cabbage cut into pieces and some meal when the pig was a bit older. A bucket-full every day or so. The bucket for the pig's food was always left under the kitchen-table and known as the slop-bucket and any leftovers from meals were thrown into it over the course of the day. Whatever was in the bucket was brought to the shed and thrown into the pig's trough every morning and afternoon. It goes without saying that the pig was always waiting eagerly for her daily feed. She alternated between being locked inside in the shed for long periods or being let out to wander the fields.

Once the pig got a bit older and stronger, they inserted one or two big rings through her snout to stop her from slamming her head against the door of the shed; the pig would get so strong after a while that there was a danger if she continued this, she'd break the door down trying to get out. The nose rings put a stop to this however. We had a special pincers to make the holes for the nose rings. Normally, it was a pair of nose rings that were put into her snout rather than a single ring and, of course, the poor pig would moan and squeal loudly while the piercing was being done. I suppose it must've been similar to someone getting pierced for a nose-ring or an earring without any anaesthetic or painkiller! That's what I'd imagine anyway. It did the job however when it came to controlling the pig's wildness or aggression. That said, I think that a certain injustice has been done to the pig over time in popular culture and she hasn't been given her due as an animal really. 'You dirty pig' is a phrase that's often used as an insult towards someone else. Or 'He's just a big pig' or 'he's just a pig of a man'. And I don't understand why this association of the pig with filth and dirt exists seeing as pigs are cleaner and far less-dirty than the majority of other animals.

For example, when you kept pigs in the shed, they'd never dirty the whole place at all like other animals but always went over to the same corner of the shed to do their business, a spot that was a good distance from where they slept. They sure did – as much as to say that this corner was their toilet – this is very different to the cow that dirties everywhere and anywhere in the shed. I don't understand therefore where that English-language phrase – 'As happy as a pig in shit' – comes from originally. The only time that I ever saw pigs deliberately getting dirty was in summer when the weather was so hot that they needed shelter or shade from the strong sun – as it's very easy for a pig to get sunburned because of its bright, white skin – unlike a calf, a donkey or a sheep! On days like that, you'd spot the pig going down into a drain or a ditch or wherever the ground was soft and rolling themselves in the mud and water to cool off. And she'd cover herself with a skin made of black mud to protect herself against the sunburn. Yes indeed – this was the factor fifteen or factor twenty the pig used on a very hot summer's day! Necessity is the mother of invention as they say, and the pig is no fool, not by a long shot.

I hope you don't mind now, if I give a short description of how they slaughtered the pig. Of course, I'll make it short, concise and to the point because it wasn't the most pleasant thing in the world. I don't think that pigs are slaughtered in this way in Ireland anymore; it wouldn't be allowed as it'd be considered too cruel; that said, I'm sure that pigs are still slaughtered in this manner nowadays in plenty of other countries, particularly in poorer countries and in more remote regions of the world.

I'll begin now so. As mentioned earlier – in case I've wandered off the point a little bit – it was just before Christmas that we slaughtered the pig. My father did the job with some of the neighbours helping him. A few of us used to help him out too when we got a little bit older. They wouldn't feed the pig for a day or two beforehand so that its stomach and intestines weren't full and it was cleaned out in as far as possible; it was like somebody preparing for an operation, I suppose. This was usually done with animals and fowl when I was young. Firstly, they led the pig out of the shed to the slab or flagstone where they planned on slaughtering it, the men keeping a tight hold on it all the while. I don't think they tied the pig's feet together the way they did with a sheep or a goat that was being slaughtered. Next, my father would cut its throat with a knife that was specially-used for this job, a knife that was razor-sharp and had a two-sided blade. This knife was kept safely out of harm's way above a tall cupboard or press where it was wrapped in newspapers and stored for the rest of the year so that the children like ourselves couldn't get near it. This knife was only taken down when a sheep or goat was about to be slaughtered.

But to return to the butchering itself – I'll be as quick as I can with the rest of this account as it's the ugliest part of it. The pig would be squealing and screaming loudly when the knife was plunged into her throat and this loud squealing went on for a few minutes at least. I can't remember now how long the squealing lasted but it could be heard all over the island, I'm sure. Maybe even as far away as on the mainland too, because sound travels very clearly across a stretch of water. The blood was drained from the pig so that it went limp and stopped screaming and all the fight and strength went out of it. A bucket was placed beneath her into which they drained all the blood and they made black puddings from this later. They never collected the initial spurt of blood that came out of her but let it spill on the ground instead, and this was the tradition with every animal that was slaughtered, whether pig, sheep or goat; maybe this was a superstition or a religious tradition from ancient times – i.e., that they were offering the blood to the earth. They also kept a duck's blood having slaughtered it and made black puddings from it – but I never saw them collect chicken's blood.

Maybe chickens don't have much blood in them, I'm not sure. Slaughtering the pig was just the beginning of the work really; the next big job was to clean and scour her outside with hot, boiling water. They'd have big buckets of boiling water ready beforehand and they'd shave every rib of hair off her with sharp knives, three or four men working as one, scraping and scouring so that you wouldn't end up with the 'hairy bacon' that's mentioned in some of the old songs for your dinner a few months later! Then they carried the pig into the shed and hung it from the ceiling by her back legs. Her back legs would be nearly touching the roof of the shed and her snout dangling just centimetres from the ground. They would take up the razor-sharp knife used for the slaughtering once more and slice through the flesh, opening the pig from the back legs down to the ribs. All the innards would come tumbling out all at once, the entrails falling out one after another in a giant mass of colour. There would be a rotten stink off them as two people held an old bathtub directly beneath the pig to make sure and catch all the warm steaming innards as they fell. These innards were later thrown out. My father normally did this part of the job himself, all the while ensuring that nothing edible was thrown out. The heart, the liver and the kidneys were kept, for example, but the large and small intestines and the lungs were thrown out. Much of the white fat was kept as this was useful for roasting meat, instead of butter. Next, they cut through the ribs with a saw. This was a tough enough job, a job for someone strong.

Once fully cleaned-out, the pig was left hanging in the shed for a few days. One or two sticks were inserted into its stomach between the ribs, to keep the carcass open, and the doors of the shed firmly shut to keep out any cats or dogs. A few days later, the meat was salted. The pig was cured and placed in a timber barrel. My father did the salting, and a couple of us gave him a helping hand. He already had a large bag of rough, raw salt ready for the job; next, they sliced the pig up into pieces, both large and small, using a saw to cut through some of the strongest bones, the spine in particular. Plenty of salt was applied to the individual chunks of meat, which were then packed tightly into the wooden barrel and this meat was one of our main food staples for the rest of the year. We always gave some joints of meat to the others in the village, especially the neighbours who'd helped us out slaughtering the pig. No part of the pig ever went to waste, not even the crubeens or trotters, each of which were carefully cleaned and eaten later. The crubeens were mainly soft fat or lard but you did find the odd sliver of meat here and there in them, little cuts that were really nice and tasty. They were very popular with people at the time but you don't see them being sold in many shops now. Indeed, when I was a boy there was a woman in Galway city known as Nora Crúb because she sold a lot of crubeens from a meat-shop on Sea Road. These types of shops are not very plentiful for years now on this side of the world, but you do see crubeens and indeed pigs' heads for sale in meat shops, on stands and on the streets of many Asian countries still today. The sight of them on a visit to that part of the world always brings me back along memory lane.

Another thing we did with the salted portions of meat was wrap them in newspaper, hang them from the ceiling in the kitchen, and leave them there until we needed to cook them. I'm not sure how long the meat remained fresh in this way; a few months, I suppose. The meat was probably also being smoked over the open fire in the kitchen all the while, of course. Yes indeed, I'm always reminded of this smoked meat when I see big large cuts of meat hanging from hooks in the ceilings of butcher shops in Spain and on the continent.

While my father did most of the salting and curing, my mother made the black pudding from the pig's blood collected during the slaughtering process. This blood was left in the bucket for a day or two afterwards and then my mam made the black puddings. I have to admit that I can't remember exactly now what else was mixed in with the black pudding but there was certainly some bread; small pieces of white loaf from the shop was mixed through it as well as oatmeal, onions, salt and pepper. One or two other ingredients may have been added to the mix, e.g., some pig-fat, but these were the main ingredients. They mixed them all through the blood in a white enamel bucket. They stood this bucket into a big pot of hot water and boiled it up. Later again, when we had a range at home, my mother baked the mixture in the oven, as you would a cake. They were the nicest black puddings I ever tasted, especially when fried up in thick black slices on the open frying pan.

Yes, indeed! We always had plenty to eat at Christmastime, and through the rest of the year also, the majority of the food provided by ourselves, so that we were almost entirely self-sufficient. This was the same for most of families in Inis Treabhair and in Connemara generally back then. For Christmas dinner, we usually had a turkey that we bought in. We never reared a turkey in our house for some reason. The odd year we'd have a goose for dinner that we reared ourselves; in addition, we had hens and ducks that we slaughtered at different stages over the rest of the year.

A week or two before Christmas was also when packages began to come in the post to us from England. The 'parcels' as we called them. They'd be outfits in them mainly and it was our aunts in England who sent them to us. Usually they were clothes their children had grown out of and didn't need anymore, but they might as well have been new, they were in such good nick. As children, we were always thrilled when these parcels arrived, the brown paper wrapped thickly around a big box and tightly knotted with white string and plastered with lots of foreign stamps. In addition to clothes, the presents often included comics, games and books – and Christmas puddings sometimes also.

My father had four sisters, each of whom emigrated to England, a fact that meant we have English rather than American cousins! It was to the US that the two generations before them had emigrated and chances are that my aunts would've gone there also if it wasn't that America was closed off to Irish immigrants by the time the eldest of them, Nan, had to take the boat. That was around the time of the First World War I believe, and a friend of hers then working in England invited her to join her over there. It was only natural that her sisters would follow her over also after that. Maybe she'd have gone to England anyway. I don't recall that there was much contact between us – or the generations before us – with the people who went to America. It was only very rarely that one of them would come back on a visit and I don't remember letters or Christmas cards being sent home from the US much either. We'd pictures hanging on the wall in our house of a few of our American cousins. One of them by the name of Father Michael Walsh was my father's first cousin, and he was the president of Boston College for a number of years. We'd certainly heard about this. Other than the occasional visitor who made the long journey from the US looking for information about their ancestors, we had very little contact with our relatives in the US. We knew of them, that's all.

Even just a few short years ago when the then US President Barack Obama chose Joseph Dunford Junior as chairman of the joint chiefs of staff – the highest role in the American Military – I didn't know of this man's existence at all – this despite the fact that I'm actually quite closely-related to him, a second cousin. In fact, I'd never have heard of him at all if it wasn't that various journalists from Raidió na Gaeltachta hadn't made enquiries with me about him and some of his other relatives in Connemara. Since then, I've met his brothers and various other relatives who've visited Ireland in recent times and I even met Joseph Dunford Junior's father, who's in his late-nineties, when on a visit to America myself a few years back. It's much easier now of course to find relatives via the Internet and keep in touch with people via the various modern-day social media. We can 'get to know' new found relatives quite easily these days but of course nothing like this existed back in the 1960s; indeed, people didn't have as much time to explore such possibilities either. There was nothing other than the odd letter, separated by long intervals of time, a letter that might sometimes take a month or more to travel from one side of the world to the other. But even if such letters were very infrequent, they were still greeted with great anticipation and joy when they did arrive.

My aunts who went to England did well for themselves over there – and three of them lived to be well into their nineties. They came back to Ireland regularly on visits and we always had a great welcome for the parcels they sent home to us every Christmas and at other times of the year sometimes also. We couldn't wait to try on the clothes, irrespective of whether they fitted us or not, or whether they were in fashion at the time. We wouldn't have known the difference anyway. The clothes they sent were always new and clean and that's all we cared about to be honest. They were shop-bought clothes too at a time when we were more used to wearing homemade fare. My mother made all the pullovers, socks and woolly caps for us then. There weren't many women of that generation who hadn't the skills to knit and crochet as well as to do sewing and darning jobs also.

OUR LOCAL postman, Muiris Ó Loingsigh from Béal an Daingin (Bealadangan) always got a great welcome whenever he came to the island. Everyone knew him by the English version of name – i.e. Maurice rather than the Irish version. 'Ar tháinig Maurice?' (Did Maurice come?) the people would always say and there was only one Maurice that they had in mind, as there was no one else on the island who went by that name. In fact, Muiris or Maurice wasn't even a particularly common name on the mainland or anywhere in Connemara at the time, and it isn't to this day either.

Maurice didn't call to the island on a daily basis because he wasn't obliged to do so as part of his job; he normally called two or three days a week. His visits were entirely dependent on the weather, of course. If the weather was too rough, we never expected him. He usually travelled from the mainland to Inis Treabhair in a currach that he borrowed from my father. My father rowed across the bay to the mainland nearly every single day doing work of one kind or another – or sometimes he went over simply because he wanted to be going places. Another reason that the postman didn't come to the island too often was that he sometimes didn't have any letters for the tiny population on the island. And it was a lot of trouble to row a currach across the sound just for the sake of a few letters. As with every postman though, Maurice was always very busy at Christmas with letters and cards from abroad for people on both the island and the mainland. Letters and cards sent from America and England mainly but the odd one from Australia also. You can be sure that there was money in some of these letters too, sent to help-out various relatives at home. Maurice was a very easy-going and friendly man, but he died from cancer in 1973, aged just fifty-eight. His brother Petey continued delivering the post to the island and surrounding areas for a good many years afterwards.

3

CHRISTMAS PREPARATIONS

There's a lot of fuss and palaver about Christmas shopping these days. You hear talk of Christmas even before Halloween has come around and no sooner is Halloween over but they never let up talking about Christmas and there's huge marketing and commercialism associated with it. This wasn't the case when I was child. In fact, there was little mention of Christmas until after the Feast of the Immaculate Conception. This feast-day falls on 8 December, and it was when it had passed that people began planning ahead for Christmas. There was extra shopping involved even if it was nothing compared to what goes on today. You have to remember also that any shopping done had to be carried in bags or boxes on the mainland initially and then across the sea to the island. Because this involved extra work, people normally only bought what they needed and very few extras.

Of course, people always made certain that they had plenty of food in for Christmas. Homemade cakes are what we nearly always had in our house but as we really loved shop-bought bread we usually bought loaves of bread and barmbracks from the shop at Christmas-time. We normally bought in plenty of raisins, sultanas and other ingredients for making cakes also. We also had treacle cakes at Christmas, my mother shopping for everything related to the cooking and the baking. They'd do one big shopping day in Galway city at least and then smaller shopping expeditions to the local shops in Connemara. We'd buy boxes of biscuit at this time of the year also. The tin boxes of USA biscuits were very popular, seeing as they had a good mixture of biscuits in them, all of them nice and sweet. These were divided out two or three biscuits per person and you made them last as long as possible. A box nearly lasted a full week for us, unlike today when everyone, young and old, is munching on biscuits all through Christmas! My mother had a saying back then – 'do bhoiligín brocach' or 'do bhoiligín santach' (you little greedy gut) for any of us who were too greedy or trying to gobble down too many biscuits or sweets.

That time you'd to ask for permission if you wanted biscuits or sweets, of course. And I don't remember any of us swiping them without permission or even thinking about that to be honest. Stealing was a sin and this was a time when the majority of people, whether young or old, believed that sin really existed. And that sins should be avoided because you'd pay for them in the next life otherwise. If I wanted to get something sweet to eat, my trick was to put my younger sister – she was three years younger than me – on the case. I'd get her to ask my mother for sweets even if she wasn't looking for them herself – or to put the idea into mam's head at least. There was a better chance that my mother would give into her anyway and I'd do all right out of it in the end. The variety of biscuits available was fairly limited, except for Christmas and other special occasions. And there weren't that many special occasions other than the stations, or when visitors called to us during the summer. The two most common types of biscuits were Marietta and Goldgrain. I'd have been about seven or eight before the Chocolate Goldgrains came out – or before I saw them for the first time anyway – and we were in heaven if we got some of them. We had cream crackers all right even though they weren't biscuits technically-speaking as dramatist Martin McDonagh might say, they were as good as biscuits to us at the time. When I went to secondary school, as a boarder in Coláiste Éinde after this, I got to know lads from the Aran Islands for the first time, and I was confused for a while before I realised that they referred to every type of biscuit as a 'cracker' – a term that we didn't use at all in Inis Treabhair – in much the same as way as Americans refer to all types of biscuit as cookies.

We always had a big cake for Christmas of course. And we never had to buy the Christmas cake or make it either because my aunt Máirín would bring one over from Bearna (Barna) for us every year. She was a great baker and cook and she used to make nine or ten cakes altogether for different people between friends and relatives. Cáit Chóil Mhaidhc from Indreabhán (Inverin) worked with her in the post office in Galway and I know that Máirín gave her a Christmas cake every year and continued this tradition for many long years, even after both women had retired from their jobs. She often gave me this cake to deliver when I was a bit older and had my own car and if Cáit wasn't home, I'd leave it into her brother – Johnny Chóil Mhaidhc's – house for her instead.

We children would put small coloured candles on our Christmas cake and light them. And sometimes, if my aunt Máirín didn't have time, we'd ice the cake ourselves as well; she'd send us over the pack of icing with the cake. I often did up the icing myself and decorated the cake with it when I got a bit older. When I was very small, my mother did this bit and I'd be the 'little greedy gut' dipping my fingers in it.

A week or two before Christmas was when we put the decorations up around the house. In truth, we didn't have that many decorations to put up and we used the same ones from year-to-year. We kept them in a box in one of the cupboards for the rest of the year. 'It's time to put up the decorations', someone would say and we'd set to work. The main ones were coloured papers and streamers folded across one another. We opened them out then like a big long accordion – four long chains of them strung out like a diamond between the four walls of the house. We also had multi-coloured balloons that we blew up and hung all around the house. We'd set a small crib that we bought in a shop on one of the shelves or in some other central place in the house and surround it with some decorations – strings of ivy that grew plentifully on the walls of the old houses on the island or holly with red berries that my father got on the mainland. I don't remember that any red-berried holly grew anywhere on the island.

Next, we'd put up the Christmas cards, stringing them in a line from wall to wall across the house or lining them up on the mantelpiece or anywhere else there was some room. If the door opened suddenly on a windy day, half of them might end up flying up into the air. We'd receive about fifty cards every year, many of them from our relatives in England – and with little expressions inscribed on them such as 'across the miles for Christmas Day'. A card would always come from France also, from a businessman whom my father sold periwinkles to over there, a man by the name of Mr Goubert. My mother would make a brown soda bread cake that she'd send over to France to him every year also, just before Christmas. What condition that soda bread was in by the time it reached France is anyone's guess! We might have received a Christmas card with French on it but I don't remember any Christmas cards with Irish on them at the time. I don't remember any cards at all in the Irish language in those days, when it comes down to it.

I don't remember us having any Christmas tree when I was very small, but once I got a bit older we started putting up our own tree each year. This wasn't a proper tree really but the branches of a pine tree instead. We'd a couple of pine trees growing around the house. We'd stand a pine branch in a small timber barrel and surround it with sods of turf to keep it straight. We wouldn't have had that many decorations on it. A few pieces of coloured paper and some shop decorations, that's all.

We'd have a gold or silver star that we made ourselves on the very top of the tree. We'd cut this star out of cardboard, the cardboard that you'd find inside a package with a new-bought shirt say. And we'd have silver or gold paper twisted around it, paper we took from empty boxes of cigarettes that my uncle smoked. Players or Sweet Afton were the main brands he smoked. There weren't that many other types of cigarettes that you could buy at the time, other than maybe Carrolls, Woodbines and Major. The gold or silver paper that was inside the cover of the cigarette-box. You had to handle this paper very carefully because it was so thin that it tore very easily. You flattened the paper first by rubbing your fingers across it very carefully and then you twisted it carefully around the star, the shape of which you'd cut out of the cardboard. Depending on the paper in the cigarettes, your star was either gold or silver. It was gold from the Sweet Afton and silver paper from the Players, as far as I can remember. This did the job fine for us as we were used to this and nothing fancier. There was no mention of Christmas lights or anything as there was no electricity on the island in those days. And even if there had been, I'm not sure that anyone would've approved of having their electricity 'wasted' on Christmas lights.

These homemade decorations might've been simple or modest enough but they still created a nice Christmas atmosphere around the house. They brought life to the kitchen of the house and we associated fun and games and pastimes with them too. A time for playing games and for relaxing a bit and a break from the constant farm-work we children did for the rest of the year. Back then, children were given a lot more work to do than today, including farm work and various jobs around the house. Christmas was a way of lighting up the darkness of winter and forgetting the short days and the cold and rain that was the norm at that time of the year. Christmas was a form of freedom and a break from lessons, homework and school.

I used to really hate it when the decorations were taken down after Christmas. The way that the house looked so joyless and bare and the cold empty feeling that you were left with afterwards. The end of Christmas meant the end of the holidays and the time for fun and games was over for the most part. It also meant the end of the family being together as the eldest of us returned to boarding school straight after Christmas. But the worst blow of all; we were going back to school and classes, back to the tables, poems and Christian doctrine and everything that needed learning off by heart.

And these had all been the furthest things from your mind just a fortnight earlier – so far away that you thought they'd never happen.

4

CHRISTMAS EVE

Certain aspects of Christmas Eve are the same in nearly every part of the world, it doesn't matter whether you're living on a small remote island such as Inis Treabhair or you're in Dublin or an enormous city the likes of London, New York or Mexico City. Santa Claus does his rounds of every village, town and city on Christmas Eve, come what may. He always shows up. Indeed, there were times on Inis Treabhair when Santa even called to us the night before Christmas Eve believe it or not. Patience and I'll explain the reason for this to you shortly – or I'll give a guess for why Santa called to us early sometimes.

As for Christmas Eve itself, we always looked forward to it with great excitement, the same as children the world-over. It was the high point of the year for us, the apex of our childhood innocence. We often lit the lamp a bit earlier than normal on Christmas Eve. Someone would say it was time to light the lamp and next thing it was glowing brightly and would remain lit for the rest of the night. It is no harm recalling again that we had no electricity on the island so that it was never as simple as pressing a button on the wall to have the light switched on or off. It wasn't that simple at all – far from it.

We only lit the lamp in the kitchen once it was fairly late in the evening and we were sure that it was needed. Likewise, the lamp wasn't quenched until the last person was going to bed in our house, sometime between 10 and 11 o'clock in the night.

We had a gas lamp in the kitchen of our house and it was only when I was a little bit older that we placed a similar lamp in the sitting room or in 'an seomra mór' (the big room) as we called it. These lamps emitted a good light. In the absence of electricity we bought in cylinders of gas regularly, one of which would be connected to the cooker for the cooking, even if much of the cooking was done over the open fire or on the range when we got one later on. We'd have another gas barrel connected to the light. The gas would last for a good while and it was only once you saw the glow of light weakening and dimming that you knew the gas in the barrel was coming to an end. One of us then turned the barrel on its side and swung it from side to side every now and then when we needed to make the light brighter and use up whatever gas was left. We were always careful and sparing with the gas, needless to say. We'd always have an extra cylinder of gas on-hand just in case – because it'd be a bad show to run out of gas either day or night when you were in on the island. These gas cylinders were heavy enough to carry when they were full and my father bought most of them from Tigh Phaddy King – later known as Siopa an Phobail – in Indreabhán. My father always kept a few spare cylinders of gas in the back of his van as people from the islands and the mainland bought them from him sometimes. It wasn't always easy for people to get them home from the shop without any method of transport and my father was able to help them out on that score.

I'm gone off on a bit of a tangent again now and you might think that I've spent enough time going on about cylinders of gas. There's a reason for this however, given that gas cylinder were so essential and important to every household on the island. Put it like this – imagine that you had a sudden power cut in your house today and you were left without any electricity for a day or two, and maybe for a long winter's night at that! This is why people were so careful and sparing with the gas and that they'd never light the lamp at home until it was well past time for it.

The gas lamp was hung from the ceiling in the middle of the kitchen in most houses and usually it had two thin chains hanging out of it, one that you pulled to turn it on and the other to turn it off. The lamp had a thing called a mantle inside in the middle of it; you lit this with a match but you'd to be very careful not to touch against it at all as it was very sensitive so you could perforate it and it would fall apart very easily. You had to change these mantles once or twice a year all the same as a hole would develop in them and they'd fall apart sooner or later. Around this mantle was a globe that acted as a protection for it, a globe that looked like a big jam jar, the bottom of which had been removed. Sometimes they broke or split and you had to get a new globe then.

To light the lamp, you had to twist the button on the lid that secured the top of the gas cylinder and this turned the gas on. You lit it then by striking a match or using an ember from the fire. Often, we used strips of torn newspaper as a light taper by twisting them tightly around one another so that they didn't burn down too quickly and singe your fingers. You lit this taper from the fire and used it to light the gas lamps also. This was so that we saved on the use of matches. 'Spare the matches', we were often told, and it wasn't that we didn't have enough money to buy them; instead, it was seen as a bad job if we ran out of matches, and the sea between us and the shops where we could buy more of them. After all, they were needed to light the cooker first thing in the morning, to boil the kettle or to light the fire if there were no burning embers left in the grate from the night before.

Those gas lamps gave off good light though, no doubt

about it. There was a special glow or warmth to them in some way. I suppose the lighting of the lamp signified that work was over for another day, the work outdoors anyway.

We also had other types of lamps in the house. We lit the Tilley lamp the odd time if we hadn't enough gas for the one of the sitting room. We'd a lantern at home that my uncle used most nights in winter when he went out to the cowshed to milk the cows or if a cow was due to calve or some other job needed doing outside. The lantern had a wick and a globe as protection from the weather so that it could be used outside at any time. We had oil in a jar at all times too as this was what we used to light the fire in the morning before there was any talk of firelighters.

And we had candles of course also, the white candles usually as opposed to the big red candle that we got in especially for Christmas. We used these candles every night for light in the bedrooms when we were going to sleep. You always had to be very careful with them however and I think my family were delighted when the torches or the flash lamps – as we called them – became more common and cheaper to buy.

Still, you had to keep the flash lamps topped up by battery regularly and we were warned to be sparing with them too. That said, they were far handier and easier to use than the candles, you had instant light from them and you weren't messing around with matches and the like.

Another big plus they had – and one that I secretly took advantage of myself – was that you could read a book under the blankets any time with them unknown to everyone else, if you were clever about it. So long as no one noticed the battery fading, that is. Once the battery was nearly gone, the light would start to flicker and weaken and you often had to take the battery out and warm it next to the fire to get a bit more life out of it – or at least that's what we thought anyway.

But we were discussing Christmas Eve so we should return to the candles that had such importance and beauty about them on that special night. The candles had a unique place and symbolism when it came to Oíche Chinn Bhliana (New Year's Eve) or Oíche Nollag Beag (Little Christmas Eve) – as the same feast day was known. These were the only occasions that candles were lit for the sake of lighting them! This was the case on Inis Treabhair at any rate! Other than the holy candles that were lit on the day of the stations or at funerals or wakes or if somebody was sick or dying or seeking a special prayer or favour – a pass in one of their exams say! This was very different from nowadays when candles are lit to create a special ambience, to add to the romance of the occasion, or to give a spicy or pungent odour or perfume to the air or to ensure positive and joyful feelings in both body and mind. Other than the large red candle that we always left on the kitchen table, it was white candles that we normally had in the different rooms of the house. These candles weren't always placed in the windows of the rooms necessarily. As long as you made sure they were placed in a safe place, this was the most important thing of all. Given that there were curtains on all the windows, light, lace curtains and heavier drapes, you had to be very careful where you positioned the lighted candles at all times.

I often read that it was the custom for people in other rural areas to cut a hole in a turnip and fix the candle into it to use for light but I never saw this done in our house. It's not that we didn't have turnips – because we did – but I'd imagine that my family didn't want any good turnips going to waste in this way. We had two candlestick holders at home that we used for the days when the stations were held in the house. They weren't enough to cover every room in the house though so we also used empty cans as candlestick holders, tin cans that'd once contained beans or peas. Re-using old tin cans in this way was a form of natural recycling, I suppose, before the contemporary concept of recycling had even been invented. Necessity is the mother of invention – as the saying goes. We used these same tins as candlesticks-holders by stuffing pieces of newspaper into the bottom of them to keep the candle steady; and you continued raising the candle in the tin-can according to how much of it was left to burn down. We'd have a candle lit in every room of the house. 'Check on the candles', we'd be told and I was often given this responsibility myself. Every hour or so, you'd go from to one room to the next and check that the candles were all standing straight and there was no fear of them falling to the side or causing a fire. They didn't need to tell me to check on the candles usually to be honest. I just did it off my own bat anyway. These lighted candles were an essential aspect of the excitement and the magic of the festivities come every Christmas Eve. They used to be always white candles but we would get one big special red candle which would be lit in the middle of the kitchen table at Christmas.

As regards the tin cans we used these same tin cans as saucepans also for boiling eggs in from time to time. You didn't cut the lids off these cans completely but left them hanging and twisted the sharp edges down and then turned them in so that you didn't cut your hand and that you had a good grip or 'handle' on your saucepan. Except that you had to be very careful once the eggs were done as the tin-lid 'handle' was always burning-hot. You had to wrap a cloth around your hand before you could even think of touching the top of the can.

It was the arrival of Father Christmas or Santa – as we called him – that we children were always most excited about. I suppose that it's the same for children all over the world. Santa normally travelled to the island by helicopter from what we heard. There was no way that his reindeers could've swum across the bay in such wintry conditions. There must've been something magical about Santa's helicopter because we never heard it and most helicopters makes a huge amount of noise. As with us islanders, Santa must've been worried about the bad weather because there was once or twice when he arrived to Inis Treabhair the night before Christmas Eve. Yes indeed. It must've been the bad weather because Santa – above anyone in the world – couldn't ever have got confused about a date as important as Christmas Eve. He was just making absolutely sure that he looked after the children of the island. Similar to the way that votes are cast on some islands these days a day or so before an official election day so's to ensure that all votes are included in the count and every single person's voice gets a fair hearing. But anyway – as children, this meant that we were sometimes keeping an eye out for Santa even the night before Christmas Eve as well as on Christmas Eve itself. Still, it was on Christmas Eve that Santa arrived nearly always. Indeed, we'd be listening to him on Radio Éireann even before his arrival as there was always a live programme with Santa broadcast earlier in the afternoon. It was from between four and five o'clock in the evening that Santa would be listing the names of the children in Ireland that he'd be calling into with presents later that night. This was provided the children were in bed early or asleep early. Not that Santa ever mentioned us in

Inis Treabhair at any stage! But then again, I suppose he couldn't mention every single child in Ireland in fairness, now could he?

Unlike in other places, we didn't go to sleep on the island until after Santa had arrived. And there were few Christmas Eve's that he didn't arrive to the island before eight or nine o'clock in the evening. We'd be warned to stay as quiet as we could and no matter what – to steer clear of the windows so that there was no danger that Santa spotted us awake through them. The odd time we'd go upstairs and hide in one of the bedrooms as quite as mice so that Santa would never know that we weren't already asleep. And the odd time we might be waiting for an hour two, or even longer for his arrival before one of the adults told us that they'd heard some kind of a noise outside a little while earlier – and that maybe it was Santa. One of us might make a quick circuit of the house then to see if he'd arrived. Sometimes it was a false alarm and he wouldn't have arrived at all but we could check on this at regular intervals.

Santa didn't leave the bag of presents in the same place for us every year; sometimes he left them in the doorway or by the windowsill, or even next to the gate outside in front of the house somewhere. It didn't matter really as long as that big bag of parcels appeared in the end and we were always so excited at the sight of it! We'd bring it inside and put it in the middle of the floor and then everyone would be tearing at the bag and emptying out its contents on the floor mad with excitement and joy. Santa would have written each of our names on the presents so that there'd be no fighting or arguing about them. And even today, fifty years later, at a time when there are so many different types of presents available, children still get similar types of presents to the ones that Santa brought us back then. Games like Ludo, Snakes and Ladders, Monopoly, story books and colouring books, plastic footballs, guns and caps, marbles, jigsaw puzzles, cards, dolls and the like. Sewing sets for embroidery and knitting. Little toy cars, etc. There were never any presents left for us that worked with a motor or with batteries though. There weren't that many of them available at the time anyway and even if they were, I suppose that Santa knew that they weren't suitable for people like us who lived on an island given that they'd be no good to us once the batteries were used up and we were so far away from the shops. And Santa certainly didn't want to make any trouble for our parents in this regard. We'd spend the rest of that night and a lot of Christmas break having fun with these new toys we'd been given.

Then, one year when I was little bit older, it was a box of jigsaw puzzles that Santa brought me as a present. I loved jigsaws, and I was very good at putting the pieces together and I suppose that Santa probably knew this!

64

Last man standing. The last islander who stood his ground until the end. Pádraig Ó Loideáin or Patsy Lydon as he was better-known with his dog outside his house in 1998. He died on 5 August, 2019. (Photo with the permission of Bob Quinn)

Patsy Lydon on the slip at Eanach Mheáin bringing the Christmas Tree into Inis Treabhair in 1991. Inis Treabhair can be seen in the background and behind that again is Cnoc Chill Chiaráin. (Photo with the permission of Joe O'Shaughnessy)

My grandmother Mary Mhicil Breathnach, from Leitir Calaidh originally. A photo of her taken in America. It is unclear who the man in the chair is. One of her relatives most likely.

My father as a young man.

My parents on their wedding day outside Saint Joseph's church in Galway city. Bearna (Barna) church was closed at the time as it was being renovated. My uncle Pádraig Ó Conghaile, who lived with us, and my aunt Eileen Ní Iarnáin from Bearna, stood (as witnesses) with my parents on the day.

The house I was raised in on Inis Treabhair.

With my mother and my sister Bridie in Knock.

Me as a little pudgy fellow in my mother's arms. This picture was taken on the island sometime during the 1960s. As we are all neatly-dressed in our Sunday-best, this photo was probably taken on a Sunday or else on a day when we had visitors.

The family on one of our trips to Knock.
In the back row are Pádraic, Máirín and Tomás. Middle row: Colm, Tadhg and Sibéal. Myself and Bridie in the front. This photo was taken in An Teach Dóite/ Maam Cross.

On my Holy Communion Day, 1969.

We've the hay saved. Me in the middle with my brother Pádraic and Proinsias Ó Catháin.

Bringing the hay in. I'm on the top of the haycock with my father. We'd save at least five or six big cocks of hay like this every year.

My father in the pucán.

Me leaving the island in the currach as a teenager.

A picture of the island people taken by the then bishop of Galway, Michael Browne on Confirmation Day, during the 1950s. Sonaí Chóilín is the first person (on the left) in the photo and the parish priest of Leitir Móir, Fr Thomas Walsh is the person standing on the extreme right of the photo.

The last van my father owned when it was beginning to fall apart. He used it for work when buying periwinkles and carrageen in the areas between Ceantar na nOileán over to Cois Fharraige and as far out west as Ros Muc.

Nóra Joe Bheairtle Uí Mhullaoidh, from an Trá Bháin originally, who married into the island. A noted sean-nós singer and a great storyteller who can often be heard on Raidió na Gaeltachta. She celebrated her ninetieth birthday in 2022.
(Photo with the permission of Scott Hedlund)

Fr Michael P. Walsh, my first cousin once removed, who was a president of Boston College between 1958 and 1968.

Joseph Dunford Junior, a second cousin of mine who was joint chairman of the chiefs of staff of the United States Military from 2015 to 2019.

A view of the island from An Ceann Thiar.

Tomás Dharach's house.

Tobar Choilmín (Little Colm's Well).

Me pictured with the other Micheál Ó Conghaile from the island on the quay-side at Inis Treabhair, 26 August, 2022.

The island schoolhouse after its renovation.

While Fr Michael Brennan was parish priest in Leitir Móir, he initiated the tradition of saying mass every summer on the island and on the other islands of the parish, a tradition that has continued to this day.

This occasion is always a great opportunity for the people of the island and their relatives and friends to return to Inis Treabhair. It is also a great chance for people who've never been previously to visit and explore the island. To the left of Father Brennan is an tAthair Johnny Ó Conaola, a second cousin once removed of mine, from Doire Choill.

Sonaí Mhicil Mharcaisín's house.

But the thing that I noticed the most was the way that Santa had written my name on the box. It was very like the writing of a sister of mine who was a few years older than me I thought. But I said nothing about this. Why would I? After all, Santa has to write thousands of names down on presents and I suppose this job becomes so boring after a while that he likes to change his writing style regularly so's to keep things interesting. And even though he has plenty of assistance with this from different helpers, I think he prefers to write the name of every single child down personally – if he has time to do them all before Christmas Eve. Even nowadays, when Santa has access to every sort of technology and computers to make his life easier, he still prefers to write the name of every child out with a fountain pen or a biro, as this ensures that his present is more individual and more personal.

One day a brother of mine who was a little bit older than me told me that there was no such thing as Santa. I remember being really disappointed on hearing this and maybe a bit angry too. And I didn't believe him then and I still don't! If this is the case, then I suppose there is no God either, I said to my brother challenging him right back. God and Santa were the same in many ways as I saw it. There were many similarities between them. Both were there to help you and look out for you even if you could never see them. They brought you gifts, both earthly or supernatural, they were both very fond of children and wanted children to be good. So I never believed my brother and I told him not to be making a fool of me or teasing me. I knew that for as long as I continue to believe in Santa, he'll visit me very Christmas and that he'll always be good to me. In much the same way as Heaven is promised to whoever believes in God. That a person's faith or belief will stand to them in the end.

5

CHRISTMAS DAY

We went to mass every Christmas Day. There was hardly anyone in the parish who didn't go to mass – if they were healthy enough to get out of the house at all. To us, there was very little difference between the mass on Christmas Day and mass on every other Sunday; the only major difference really as far as I can remember was that the priest didn't give a sermon on Christmas Day. You sat down as you did on any Sunday when it was time for the sermon. We'd only be sitting down for half-a-minute though when the priest would invoke the blessings of Christmas on the community and wish everyone a healthy, happy and blessed Christmas. And a prayer that everyone would be alive at the same time the following year. That was it; everyone who was sitting down got to their feet again and the priest continued with the creed and with the rest of the mass. We weren't complaining.

We always looked forward to going to mass for other reasons also. It was a kind of 'a day out' for us really, an excuse for us to leave the island for part of the day at least. For some of the islanders, it was the only time of the week that they travelled over to the mainland Most families didn't go out shopping except maybe once or twice a week, and usually it was one or two members of the family who did this task. So even if we weren't always that keen on going to mass, we were keen to leave the island for a while anyway, and it was a change from the everyday work and humdrum of island life generally. As you'd imagine, the latter could be boring enough at times as there was little change from one day to the next.

Travelling from the island to the mainland for mass at Christmas time was like any other Sunday during the year in many ways therefore. One thing that we always made sure of was that we were in time for mass, the 11 o'clock mass in Séipéal Leitir Móir (Lettermore church). We always wore our best clothes, our Sunday clothes as they were called, and everyone was scrubbed clean from the day before. We left the house at 10 o'clock in the morning and it took five or ten minutes to make our way over to the South Pier. We made our way across the bay in a three-seated currach usually and we'd bring coats to place beneath us in the boat. No matter how fine the day looked on departure, you never left the island without a coat with you. Others brought newspapers to place beneath them to make sure their Sunday clothes didn't get dirty. We'd have some of our neighbours in the curragh with us sometimes but not that often – as there were enough of us in the currach as it was. Rather than going to the Céibh Eanach Mheáin (Annaghvaan Quay), some of the island people travelled over to Brandy Harbour as the walk from there to the church in Leitir Móir was much shorter. Our family always went to Eanach Mheáin however and it took about a quarter of an hour of rowing. It was two men rowing usually and we'd a van which we left parked in a shed in Eanach Mheáin from which it'd take my father about fifteen minutes to drive into Leitir Móir. We'd reach Leitir Móir usually at about 10:45 a.m. where we parked the van next to Nicko Ó Conchubhair's store there. That store was where Tigh Ruairí Uí Chonchubair's supermarket is today and we always parked up there. Some of the Eanach Mheáin people would come in the van with us there as many families didn't have their own cars at the time. Some of the people travelled to mass by motorbike or push bike then while others walked to the church.

There was no midnight mass – or Aifreann na Gine, as it was called – held in Leitir Móir then. I'd reached my teens probably before the parish priest there – Father Whelan – initiated this custom in the 1970s. But even if there had been a midnight mass held there before this, it wouldn't have suited the islanders very well and especially the island children to be travelling by boat at night in the pitch dark. But midnight mass did suit the

69

people on the mainland – and another group of people also – the stragglers who wandered home from the pubs on Christmas Eve with a fair load of drink on them. And no hurry on the same crowd getting out of bed the following morning either. There was always a gang of them in the back of the church who were fairly well-on it too sometimes – so much so that the priest threatened to put an end to the Aifreann na Gine one year completely, if the same crowd didn't behave a bit better from then on.

I think that the way this problem was solved eventually in Leitir Móir – and maybe in some other parishes also – was to close the pubs earlier on holy Christmas Eve night. They closed them around 9 o'clock from then on, and you can be sure that there were some people – between drinkers and bar owners – who weren't too happy about this arrangement either. People normally acceded to the wishes of the priest back then however. This change in routine made no difference to the islanders as there was no pub on the island anyway – even if some people saw nothing wrong with going out for a drink on Christmas Eve before mass. Not that people ever drank much on the island as it wasn't easy to bring alcohol in onto the island anyway. If someone liked their drink, it was as easy for them to have a few on the mainland and bring it onto the island in their stomach or on their person – provided that they were able to hold their drink.

We never drank much in our house anyway, even if we always had some alcohol in just in case. Even at Christmas-time, hardly anyone in our house took a drop - not unless a visitor or a neighbour arrived in. My father would take a drink but only when he was on the mainland and at the end of a day's work. He'd usually have a few pints in Michael Jack's – in Eanach Mheáin. John Michael Jack – was a first cousin of his once removed. Three or four pints is what he usually drank. Máirtín Tom Sheánín, who served pints there as a young lad, used to say that my father would drink his pint in four long drinks, even if there were long intervals between each of them. My mother was never against drink herself but then she was never in favour of it much either – just so long as people didn't go overboard with it. There'd been ten children in her own family and she had a short verse that was true in relation to them:

There are five of us who'd never take a drop.
And five others who could drink plenty …

I'm not going to mention any names here now as all of these people have moved on, God rest them. Suffice to say, that my mother belonged to the group cited in the first line of this verse and the five people mentioned in the second line drank their share fairly often and made up for the other five who didn't drink at all.

We always had plenty to eat at Christmas time as outlined earlier and Christmas dinner was the biggest meal of the year. We had turkey for dinner that day. Outside of Christmas, we rarely ate turkey, if at all. But it was the lovely stuffing that my mother made for the occasion that I liked best of all and it was only at Christmas that we had this, as far as I can remember. For dessert, we'd have Christmas pudding and custard followed by tea, Christmas cake, biscuits and chocolate sweets.

Christmas Day was a fairly quiet day in many ways. Relatives wouldn't visit that day as this wasn't practical on an island, given the time of the year. I don't remember the neighbours calling into us or that we'd call to them either that day. It was a day for the family really, I suppose, and I don't remember that we went outdoors a whole lot that day. The crowd who were a bit older than us would venture out all right on Christmas Day night to look for the wren in preparation for the following day. A few of the neighbours often joined them in hunting the wren. They'd bring torches with them and they'd usually find a wren in one of the sheds or outhouses somewhere and keep him in a jam jar for the following day.

'It's Christmas all year round' they say these days. It's one of those sayings that's come to the fore over the last generation or two, but I think that the saying itself is dying out now as the older people who saw both worlds pass on, those people who saw a life of poverty when they were young and a life that improved greatly as they became older. Of course, as this saying implies people are far better off nowadays and aren't short of anything all-year-round. When the older generation were growing up, they weren't that well off at all, other than come Christmas-time when people always did their utmost to put the best side out. No matter how poor a family was they tried to have plenty of food and drink in for Christmas even if they had to scrimp and save for the rest of the year to make sure. There was no poverty in Inis Treabhair when I was young. They had enough and even a little bit extra for the day by the fire in most families. This was how it was, for as long as I can remember.

The main Christmas blessings that we wished on others were 'Nollaig Mhaith' or (Happy Christmas!) or 'Nollaig Mhór Mhaith dhuit'. The word 'mór' (great, wonderful) was often used in relation to Christmas; people would also say: 'Mo chuid den Nollaig ort', or (My best (wishes) for the Christmas to you) while others again often uttered the phrase – 'Go mbeirimid beo ar an am seo arís' (May we be alive this time next year/May we live to see this time next year) to one another also. They probably had in mind those relatives and friends of theirs who had died since the previous Christmas.

I NEVER saw a white Christmas on Inis Treabhair during my time there, even if we were always hoping for snow – as children are everywhere that snow rarely falls. It was solely on the Christmas cards that we ever saw snow. Indeed, it's very rare for us to have a white Christmas in Ireland anyway; I must've been in my thirties before I saw my first white Christmas ever, and I was living in Indreabhán (Inverin), on the mainland by then. And I wasn't long getting tired of it either because I couldn't get out of the house for a few days with the slippery and dangerous roads. Trapped again! Marooned but not by the sea this time! Still, even if I wasn't too happy about it, I suppose Santa was delighted that year having a thick blanket of snow beneath him covering the green hills and fields of Ireland as he delivered his presents, travelling all the way by sleigh from the North Pole.

6

BETWEEN TWO CHRISTMASES

If Christmas Eve was the high point of children's lives then I think that we enjoyed the period between the two Christmases best of all. That is between the 25 December or Christmas Eve and Little Christmas Eve which falls on the 5 January. They were known as 'dhá lá dhéag na Nollag', or the twelve days of Christmas. We had a lot of free time during those few weeks, we had no school lessons and neither had we any poetry or maths tables to learn off by heart. There were no schoolbooks to be opened or essays to write. And it was the time of year when we'd the least amount of work to do in the fields or around the house outside. Even the adults didn't do a lot of work around the place at that time of the year.

We got great mileage out of the new toys and games Santa had given us instead. We always had books in our house and we read them eagerly at this time of the year. My mother always bought whatever books that Santa didn't bring us. It was rare enough for her to come home from Galway that she didn't have one or two books with her; she'd have got them in a bookshop such as Kennys usually. Of course she'd worked as a teacher herself at one stage. Actually, this was what had brought her to Inis Treabhair the first day ever – after which she'd spent three years teaching in the National School there between 1949 and 1952. When she married my father in 1952, she had to give up teaching because of the rule then that women in the civil service couldn't work when they were married. This was a ridiculous rule that the government only put an end to around the year 1973, believe it or not. Anyway, my mother inspired an interest in reading amongst us so that we were able to read for ourselves from quite a young age. And even when we could read, my mother often read a chapter or two from a book to us every night when we were gathered around the fire before saying the rosary. As far as I can remember, they were books in English that she read to us for the most part, especially the books of Enid Blyton. This included *The Famous Five* series, a series which has had new and contemporary versions of it published in recent times. These readings by the fire at night were like a soap opera to us as we eagerly awaited the next chapter in the story, the next adventure. There weren't a very wide range of books published in the Irish language at that time but she read us the few books that were available. We had Sinéad de Valera's series of fairy stories; I still remember the green and blue covers on them and the fact that they were sold for two or three pence each at the time. I remember my mother reading *Jimín Mháire Thaidhg* to us, and how much we enjoyed it. I still consider that book a classic in the Irish language. We read Mairéad Ní Ghráda's translations in the Ladybird series and my mother read *Séadna* to us when we got a bit older. I found that story both interesting and frightening at the same time. We'd lend books to other families on the island and vice-versa.

We had a gramophone at home that we listened to a lot. Or, at least, any time it wasn't broken, that is! Because it was a very fragile instrument especially in a house full of children; you had to wind it up with a metal handle. There was a hole in the side of the gramophone that you could squeeze the handle into it to wind it. The more you wound it the tighter it got, but you had to be careful not to go overboard with it or you could break the machine completely – similar to the old watches or clocks before batteries came in. Still and all, the gramophone got broken often enough. I remember my father once opening it out on the table and taking all the bits and pieces out of it. I'm not sure whether he managed to fix it that time or whether we'd to bring it into Galway city or over to Peait Tommy who lived in Indreabhán – in the place where Tír na nÓg is now – to try and get it fixed. What I do know was that this same gramophone was often brought away to be fixed and it was a big blow to us whenever it was gone – even for a week – as we had very few other ways or opportunities to listen to music or songs at the time. Normally the radio we had would only be switched on at news time.

I still remember well some of the records we had at home then, some of the heavy, old-33s that you had to be very careful that they didn't break when handling them. They were completely different from the light plastic records that came out later as specially-made for the record players. Amongst the records we had in the house were ones by Seán 'ac Dhonncha, Seán Chóilín Ó Conaire and Seosamh Ó hÉanaí (Joe Heaney) as issued by Gael-Linn. I'm not sure why, but if you look at the back of those old records today, you'll see a picture of Seán 'ac Dhonncha with one fist raised in the air; and in the case of the picture of Seosamh on the back of his record, both of his fists are closed, as if he was a boxer or something! My older brothers used to tell me that if I was bold, the singers on the records would give me a few boxes. As much as to say that they were keeping an eye on me! My brothers were probably trying to keep me away from the records so that they didn't get scratched or broken. But I must have been very young at the time to believe something as ridiculous as that! I was afraid of those singers on the records back then. Ironically enough, as things would turn out many years later – thirty years later to be more exact – I would find myself sitting in the same studio as Seán 'ac Dhonncha and Seán Chóilín Ó Conaire and recording them singing other versions of the same songs that were on the 33s – songs I'd learned off-by-heart from them so many years earlier. When I was very young, I still remember standing and staring into the fire in the sitting room at home by myself and reciting every verse of *Amhrán na Trá Báine*. I knew the whole song off by heart and, even if I wasn't a singer, I wanted to know every verse of the song off by heart – or, at least, the four verses that were on that record at the time. In truth, I knew every single bit of that song, word by word.

If it hadn't been for the Gael-Linn records, of course, we'd have had very little chance to hear any sean-nós recordings at all. We had a radio at home but we weren't allowed go near it when we were small; it was kept up high on a shelf out of harm's way so unless you stood up on a chair and stretched up as high as we could go, you couldn't get anywhere near it. There were cables and an aerial hanging out of it also and maybe that was the main reason it was kept up high and out of reach. It was rarely switched on either, except for the news. Chances are that there was only one station on it at the time anyway – Radio One or Radio Athlone as it was often called. There was no talk of Radio Luxembourg yet, a station that would prove revolutionary from a pop music point of view when I was a teenager. Nor was there any mention of Radio Two then either.

When I was seven or eight years of age, my parents bought a normal radio and I remember us listening in to the Irish-language plays of Eoin Ó Súilleabháin every Saturday night. I especially remember the different series known as *Colm sa Bhaile* and *Colm ar Strae*, etc. and there were one or two other programmes broadcast in Irish on it weekly, over time. One of these was *Aeriris* as presented by Proinsias Mac Aonghusa, a man who was a third-cousin of mine as it happens. He was a son of Criostóir Mac Aonghusa who spent a year teaching school on Inis Treabhair when my father was still at school. And there were plenty of other programmes in English that we listened to, between interviews and music and I remember this new radio being turned on far more often than the other radio. I heard songs such as Seán Ó Sé's *An Poc ar Buile* which was riding high in the charts at the time regularly on it and I remember being particularly taken with this song given how rarely you heard Irish language songs on the radio at the time.

The arrival of Raidió na Gaeltachta – or Raidió Chonamara, as it was often called locally then – in 1972, when I was ten years of age, was a major development in our lives. And even if it only broadcasted two hours a day at the beginning this was like a revolution in terms of Irish language broadcasting and we were very interested in every programme that was on it. The station spoke directly to us in a way; it was our voice and our dialect that we heard on it. In addition to chat shows and music there was a children's programme on *Sibhse, a Pháistí* with Aingeal Ní Chonchubhair. And the Munster dialect proved no obstacle to us either. It included a weekly segment of the story *Méinín agus an Madra* as written and narrated by Siobhán Ní Shúilleabháin and we eagerly awaited each new weekly episode of it, like a soap opera. The programme included different competitions that young people such as ourselves could enter and that encouraged regular listeners. I knew how to knit and crochet and I remember winning a prize for a red cap that I'd crocheted and sent into the programme. I'm not sure now whether it was 75p or £1.50 that was on the cheque that I received as a prize. I remember my father counting the money out on the table for me after he'd cashed the cheque on the mainland.

As there was no television on the island in the absence of electricity, this only increased the value and importance of the radio for us. I didn't see any television myself until I was six or seven years of age when I was on the mainland one day with my father. I think that we went into someone's house in Carraroe where a television was switched on and I couldn't take my eyes off these perpetually-moving pictures. And even if there was nothing on the television that day except motor-racing, my eyes were still glued to the screen.

Some years later, when I was a teenager, Patsy Lydon got a small television. It was a ten-inch screen television, I think, in black and white, one that ran on batteries that were almost as big as the television itself! I think it worked on car batteries that had to be brought over to the mainland regularly to be recharged. If sparing with it, the battery might last a week or two but you could always tell when it was beginning to run down as the picture on screen – or what was left of it – got smaller and smaller as the black frame around it increased. You could only get RTÉ1 of course; that was the only station available in the west of Ireland at the time. People could tune into the BBC on the mainland but only by travelling a few hours up to Athlone or the Midlands, something which people did the odd time there was a big soccer match or boxing fight on that wasn't being shown on RTÉ. Yes indeed, this was how limited broadcasting was back then and how much trouble people went to in order to watch an event that they really wanted to see, believe it or not. It was all very different from today, needless to say. As I write these memories from the 1960s and 1970s down now, I'm sitting 6,000 miles away from home in South Asia and listening to Raidió na Gaeltachta via Wi-Fi! And I can catch segments of news from TG4, a television station that's just back the road from where I live in Ireland. Isn't life strange! And what changes we've seen since those days back then and how different the world is now! To have that small television on the island, all of fifty years ago, no matter how small the picture it screened – it was a major revolution in our previously-restricted worldview.

The Ó Loideáin's or Lydon's house was the main port of call for people socialising in the evenings not only come Christmas but all-year round especially during the long winter nights. The main pastime that adults had was playing cards and there were just about enough people there in the evenings to make up a game of 25. I didn't have any interest in the cards myself but I'd go over there when I got a little bit older because I liked watching their television. The woman of the house herself – Nóirín – liked watching television too even if she understood very little English. She was fairly elderly and fragile by then and it was often hard to tell whether she was dreaming or whether she was following what was on the screen. She loved smoking a pipe and always had her pipe next to her by the hearth and every now and then you'd hear her talking to herself before she'd give a big roar of laughter! Nearly all the television programmes were in English and yet she'd hardly a word of that language, barely enough to put the dog out. We were watching a film one night when an argument started between a man and woman at the end of which the woman screeched at the man – 'Go away you bitch!' Noreen got a fright and sat bolt-upright by the corner of the fire and says 'Oh damn it to hell', but you'd swear that woman spoke Irish!

I was getting more interested in sports at the time, especially soccer, and following the matches in England regularly. Manchester United was my favourite team and still are to this day, even though they're not doing that well at the moment. George Best, from Belfast, was at the top of his game back then of course so many Irish people followed United. Others again followed Leeds United as they were in the First Division at the time. The matches were on Saturday's only at the time, all of them beginning at 3 o'clock, a fact which meant it was always half time at 3:45 p.m. or a few minutes after that. Other Saturdays of the year – other than at Christmas – if I was working out in the fields picking potatoes or the like, I'd often make an excuse to go inside and get the half-time scores on the radio, on the BBC. We could get the BBC sometimes – just about – if there was a strong battery in the radio but you'd to extend the aerial fully and twist it over and back and from side to side until you got a reasonably good signal. And once you got a strong signal, you'd no choice but to keep standing in the same spot, aerial in hand and not move at all if possible. And you were one of the lucky ones – if you got to stay inside at that time on a Saturday afternoon – because of rain, or just to get away from work. The second half of one of the matches would be broadcast live and this was a real treat for some of us if it was a United match that was being broadcast.

Soccer was another major reason that we were interested in the first television on the island. Jimmy Hill presented *Match of the Day* every Saturday night and we got to watch it a few times when we were over in the Lydon's house. We'd call in there on a visit sometimes – ('mar dhea' – supposedly!) – on certain nights in the hope of catching some of the soccer matches. I still remember being over in Lydon's one particular Saturday night and really looking forward to watching *Match of the Day*. It didn't start until late at night, around about 11:20 p.m. just after the *Late Late Show* finished on RTÉ. And just as Gay Byrne was saying goodbye and saying – 'Good night, good night' what did Patsy do but get to his feet saying 'Good night good night' back to Gay and turn off the television straight away! We were very disappointed but of course we didn't say anything. How could we? Patsy probably hadn't thought of the soccer at all and even if he had done, you couldn't really blame him for trying to save whatever was left of the battery or heading off to bed as he'd always be at Sunday mass the following morning at 9 o'clock in Leitir Móir church on the mainland.

The Lydon's house was always a very warm and

welcoming place to visit and I often called in there, the same with the other youngsters from the island along with some of the adults. The odd time, Nóirín would ask us to bring a bucket of freshwater into her from the well and we always helped her out on that score. She'd always reward us for our troubles if she'd anything nice in. She'd always make lovely tea for us and give us bread with loads of jam on it. To this day, I can still see Nóirín walking across the floor to the kitchen table, the pot of tea she'd taken down from the hearth in her hand. She had a peculiar habit – one that I'd never seen in anyone else – of holding the pot in her right hand and just her fingernails touching the heat of the bottom of the pot, so that she didn't burn herself. Yes indeed, those visits to the Lydon's house really lit up our lives; limited though they might have been – the radio and television in that house were a real eye-opener for us and a crucial link between ourselves and the outside world.

We also had newspapers on the island sometimes, needless to say. The *Sunday Independent* and the *Sunday Press* were bought every Sunday and my father bought the *Irish Independent* fairly regularly during the week. He bought the *Connacht Tribune* every week as well as the *Farmers Journal* sometimes. He got the newspaper *The Skipper* – relating to fishing and the sea – sent to him through the post and that was the lot as regards newspapers.

I'm not sure whether the *News of the World* was widely available back then but it wasn't in our house anyway. That said, as a teenager, I often heard Pat Lindsay – the former master of the High Court who built a house for himself in Eanach Mheáin when he retired and whom I often met in Michael Jack's – tell the story of how he'd been in the village shop one Sunday morning and overheard a man at the counter say: 'Give me twenty Players and a copy of that little sex-paper'.

We never had the *News of the World* at home but it wasn't long after this that we had the nearest thing to it, I suppose, the *Sunday World* that was published for the first time in March 1973. We got the first edition of it and bought it regularly after that; it goes without saying that the *Sunday World* was very different from the *Sunday Press* or the *Sunday Independent* in terms of layout, subject matter or presentation. But for young people such as ourselves, it came across as modern and attractive even from the point of view of how it was laid out and printed. It was very different in that there were colour pictures on the front and back pages and coloured pages throughout the newspaper. 'Ireland's Only Coloured Sunday' was their motto in those days and this was the truth. There were no colour pictures in any of the other newspapers, other than the *Sunday Independent* on All-Ireland Final days when they included colour pictures of the two teams and the rival captains on the front and back pages. In my mind's eye, I can still see the colour cover of the *Independent* for 1971 Galway v Offaly – the two teams pictured in full colour as well as a full-colour photo of the captains Liam Salmon whom I got to know later in my life as a teacher, and Willie Byrne. The first page of the *Indo* appeared in colour also on the day of the Carroll's Irish Open as the Irish Open golf tournament was then known, and the Irish Independent also included some picture in colour on one day towards the end of the year when they celebrated the 'sports stars of the year' awards. Other than on those few occasions, everything in the papers was black-and-white or, at least, everything else that I came across anyway.

The *Sunday World* was a real revolution in terms of publishing therefore at the time and just as it really livened up and embellished the lives of the Irish people in a number of ways it also added colour to the restricted, remote lives we had as cut off on Inis Treabhair also. We loved reading it and our enthusiasm and curiosity was only whetted by the stories it covered, as we got older. My mother always referred to it as 'an páipéirín beag' (the little paper-een) and she read bits out of it every now and then. The *Sunday World* might have been very different from the other newspapers, but I suppose my mother knew as well as we did, that it was a form of education and an eye-opener on contemporary life in Ireland as it really was then. It wasn't a very big paper, seeing as it was a tabloid but there's no doubt but that it had a wide influence across the country in those days.

In addition to the newspapers, we read comics. I don't remember that we bought them ourselves but we'd get parcels of them sent to us from cousins in Galway and London – the likes of *The Dandy, the Beano, Cor!* – and *Commando* – the latter related to war and guns and I never had any interest in it myself. A magazine that came out once a month was *Our Boys* and when we were a bit older we'd read *Ireland's Own* and *Spotlight* a magazine that related mostly to pop music; we also read two soccer magazines called *Shoot* and *Goal* and one relating to GAA games called *Solo*.

WHEN IT came to New Year's Eve, I don't remember that we had any special celebrations on the island that night. They didn't have fireworks or that sort of thing much in those days and even if they did, we wouldn't have had them in Inis Treabhair at any rate. There was no pub or hotel on the island where people could congregate for a concert or a music session and the population on the island was too small for this anyway. The odd person might have gone out socialising on the mainland that night but very few, I'd say. So New Year's Eve was mainly given over to listening to the radio and whatever fun and games we made for ourselves. Similar to Christmas Eve we lit candles in every room and we did the same again on Oíche Nollag Beag (Little Christmas Eve) on 5 January. We always referred to this latter feast day as Oíche Nollag Beag although it's also referred to as Oíche Nollag na mBan (Women's Christmas Eve) in some places also. Another name for this feast day was Oíche Chinn an Dá Lá Déag (Epiphany Eve) signifying that the twelve days of Christmas had officially come to an end. I always felt a certain sense of sadness around then as it meant the end of the holidays and the joy and ease of Christmas. One small consolation for people however, was that they knew there'd be a bit of a stretch in the evenings from then. Slowly but surely, the evenings would grow longer and brighter as time went on – even if it was only 'fad coiscéim coiligh' (lit: the length of a cockerel's step') in the first few days.

7

THE TYPEWRITER

One year, a week before Christmas, my mother returned from Galway with something that none of us was expecting, a machine that I'd never imagined we'd have under the roof our house. A typewriter! This was quite an unusual and rare device in any house in Connemara at the beginning of the 1970s or the early-1980s. I can't tell you now whether it was a brand-new one she brought home or whether it was second-hand. I'm not sure either what motivated her to buy it I don't remember any of us asking her to get one and I've no idea whether she discussed it with anyone in the family beforehand because as I was the second youngest of the eight children, she wouldn't have been talking to me about it anyway. A typewriter wasn't cheap to buy at the time, I'm certain of that. And my mother was always careful with money and wouldn't have spent it on something without thinking carefully about it beforehand and without good reason to.

If I remember rightly, my mother may have said later

that she bought it for my younger sister Bridie who was three years younger than me – as she thought she might want to write a book someday. Bridie was a voracious reader and every day, after school, she disappeared into her room where she spent most of her time reading quietly. She loved reading and read any book she came across, cover to cover. Maybe this was what inspired my mother to buy the typewriter the first day ever. She probably thought that it'd be no harm for us to have typing skills also for whatever life might hold in store for us when we finished school. My mother was someone who was always encouraging to children and younger people like ourselves and trying to help us get ahead in life. I've heard more recently – that it was actually my eldest sister Máirín whom my mother bought the typewriter for. Máirín was in secondary school at the time and learning shorthand and typing skills, both of which would've been to her advantage if she'd looked for a job in the civil service afterwards. This makes sense to me as Máirín was practising on the typewriter during the holidays and the rest of us weren't allowed to go anywhere near it either.

Whatever the story, the truth is that when the cat's away, the mice are at play! – and before long, Máirín wasn't the only one knocking sparks out of that typewriter. It was given a right pounding – and that's the only way to describe it. Because you had to give each of the keys a good strong rap or the printed letters appeared too light on the page. A good hard tap and the print was much stronger and heavier. Typewriters, such as this one, were completely different from the electric ones that became available a few years later; with the latter you barely touched the keys and they did the rest of the work for you – the letters nearly dancing by themselves in front of you and filling up the page.

Don't ask me what make the typewriter was now! I remember that it had a blue cover that was always put over it when no one was using it – to keep it safe and free of dust. It had a ribbon running across it as attached via a spool on either side, a ribbon with two colours. The lower half of the ribbon was black, the upper half was red, and there was a small lock on the side that you clicked up or down depending on what colour you needed. It was the black print that you used mainly, a fact that meant the black part of the ribbon always wore out before the red half. You used the red print then once the black was all gone and before you got a chance to replace the ribbon. After we'd all been using the typewriter a while though, all the accuracy and exactness was knocked out of the typewriter and it didn't matter what way you arranged the ribbon, the letters came out half-black and half-red across the page. We'd no choice but to put up with this or give up using the typewriter completely. Sometimes when the ribbon was too loose, the colours got all messed up as well, and over time, one or two of the keys started to jam on the top of the page or hang there in mid-air until you released them with your fingers. Of if you tapped two keys very quickly one after another, they might get twisted together – with one going up and the other coming down – tangled in one another like the two oars of a currach during a race. Eventually you had to employ a mixture of kindness and force to keep the typewriter going properly at all. My uncle wasn't too happy sometimes at the continuous racket when typing on the kitchen table and we'd have to stop typing, especially when the news came on the radio. I was probably the one who got the most use out of the typewriter. I spent a good deal of time typing up a story one Christmas – a novel as I thought myself – 'The Adventure of the Shabby Man' I titled it, and it was written in the same style as the Enid Blyton books – as carefully laid out in different chapters. I remember folding the A4 pages into four equal parts, assigning the numbers and then typing them out one after another – something that was difficult enough because I'd the paper doubled twice when I put it through the typewriter – a typewriter that was designed for A4 pages only. I stuck the pages together then until I'd made my own little book with more than forty pages; I put a cover on it that I coloured in with crayons. And where would a book be without the author's name clearly visible on the front page – 'Michael Joseph Conneely' I authored it. 1974. There was no publisher referenced for this book however! Publishers and the like weren't something that I considered much at the time obviously! There was time enough for all that! It's a very different story today! Nowadays if I pick up a book in Irish or English in a shop, I check out the name and logo of the publisher almost as quickly as I check the author or title of the book. Whatever about information on the author of the book, I attach a particular importance to the name of the publisher and often buy books based on this alone.

Who knows? Now that I think back on that fiction effort of mine when I was twelve years of age – when I didn't already know what I wanted to do with my life – that I wanted to be a writer. Because as I often say today – I've been or was on a temporary loan or sabbatical – for a very long time by now, admittedly – to the publishing business. I did all my typing with two fingers and this initial work with the typewriter surely helped set me on the journey of writing, and perhaps on the publishing road also – who knows? Now that I have written nearly twenty books – and can use all of my fingers when typing, and even though I'm still a bit slow and awkward about it – the ironic thing is that I've written the first draft of every book of mine with a pen, including this one here! I have a special affinity with pen and paper and I always will.

Anyway, I brought my newly typed book to school with me and showed it to the schoolmistress we had at the time – Seosaimhín de Róiste from Brosna in Kerry. I also had the neck to tell the teacher that it might be worthwhile to read a chapter from the book to the other pupils every day at school. I know that Seosaimhín was certainly interested in it and I remember her reading pieces of the story aloud to the school and laughing – but not laughing in a way that was insulting or anything like that. When I say – aloud to the school – rather than the class, it's because there were only about twelve pupils in the school at the time and all of the classes which averaged about two pupils were taught in the one classroom. Yes indeed. She read out sections of the book all right but she was wise enough not to read all of it. After all it was no masterpiece!

Seosaimhín was the second teacher I had on the island and she taught me for a year and three months altogether. Before her, we'd had Máire Ní Chonghaile from An Púirín, two miles west of Spiddal who spent nearly seventeen years teaching on Inis Treabhair before she transferred out to An Gort Mór in Rosmuc. Máire was an incredibly diligent and devoted teacher and I remember her talking about Pádraig Mac Piarais (Patrick Pearse) and Pádraic Ó Conaire, and telling us how they'd both been writers. I was just six or seven years of age at the time, I think, but I remember thinking that I'd never be interested in doing the likes of that myself; because I thought it was a strange thing for an adult to do – to spend their time sitting indoors writing a book, especially on a fine, sunny day. It wasn't something that I associated in any way with life or work on the island.

My mother used to tell us about Pádraic Ó Conaire as well because she had some memories of him from when she was very young. Ó Conaire had spent a while lodging in my grandmother's Sibéal Uí Iarnáin's house in an Baile Nua, in Bearna (Barna) while he was teaching on an Irish-language course in the area. My mother used to tell how he had given a manuscript to my grandmother to bring into O'Gorman's in Galway – (then situated where Eason's bookshop is today) for typing up. My grandmother used to call into Galway regularly selling butter, eggs and vegetables as did many other women from Cois Fharraige. Máirtín Ó Cadhain gives a wonderful description of these women's work in his short story 'An Bóthar go dtí an Ghealchathair' (The Road to Bright City).

As Máire Ní Chonghaile was from An Púirín originally she had a particular affinity with Máirtín Ó Cadhain and I remember her telling us about him in school when he died in 1970. I was about eight years of age at the time and I suppose this is the first time I'd paid particular attention to his name. A while later, she hung a big black and white picture of Ó Cadhain on the wall that remained there for many long years as if he was looking down at us. The motto on the picture was:

> *Sí an Ghaeilge athghabháil na hÉireann, agus is í athghabháil na hÉireann slánú na Gaeilge.*
>
> *The Irish language is the reclamation of Ireland and the reclamation of Ireland is the salvation of the Irish language.*

THE DOORS of Inis Treabhair National School were locked for the final time in the early summer of 1980 – exactly eighty years after its foundation in 1900 – with just three pupils left in the school, Réamonn, Máirtín and Gearóid Ó Mullaoidh – when the eldest of the three lads was old enough to go onto secondary school the following autumn. It was the end of an era.

The school still stands fine today, refurbished as a dwelling house by Máire and Frank Ó Faogáin, who spend time there every now and then. They are the only people who live on the island now.

8

THE DEATH OF SONAÍ CHÓILÍN

Sonaí Chóilín, the oldest inhabitant of Inis Treabhair, died just after Christmas, on 12 January, 1974, when I was just twelve. I was in his house when Sonaí died. It was a Sunday night. We were saying the rosary and he died as we were praying. This was the first time I'd ever seen someone die on the island.

Sonaí Chóilín was eighty-four years old and married to Mary Neidín Sweeney from Leitir Calaidh and they had no children. I'd known him since I was very young because he'd pay us a visit fairly regularly. He'd always call on Sunday night, as far as I can remember, every month or every six weeks or so, and himself and my father would pass the rest of the evening chatting and swapping stories together – not that the rest of us paid much attention to them at the time.

He often brought us presents on his visits too when we were small. Short trousers or short pants mainly, the same as every boy wore at the time. He'd give them as presents to other young lads on the island too. At school one day, three of us were standing up at the front desk during the catechism class but whatever turn the conversation took, or however it came up, we began discussing the clothes we wore and the trousers we had on. And we realised then that it was Sonaí Chóilín who'd given all three of us the trousers we had on. Maybe because he had no children himself, Sonaí Chóilín was always looking out for us and always bought them for us. I don't think that – or at least I can't remember that – he bought presents for the girls at all.

Over in Tigh Chonraí shop in Gairfeanach, in Rosmuc, was where he bought the clothes; this was a shop that attracted a lot of customers when I was a child. The shop was known for the fact that you could buy anything at all you needed there, from a spool of thread to an anchor for boats. I was only ever in the shop once myself. I went there with my uncle who'd call there a few times a year to buy feed for the cattle and do other shopping. This was a long time before modern shopping came. If you asked for a pound of tea or sugar for example, they'd fill it out into a brown paper bag for you, using a tiny shovel that they dipped into a big sack right in front of you for the purpose. I remember Michael Chonraí weighing it on the scales and knotting the brown paper up with string, then totting the bill up with his pen, between pounds, shillings and pence. They didn't have tills in too many places at the time so you often saw the sums added up like this on the brown paper bags that came home from the shop. There was no talk of plastic bags in those days.

It was in Tigh Chonraí that Sonaí did most of his shopping and the same went for many Connemara people at the time, never mind the island people. After all, it was far easier for people to row or sail a few miles across the water – by boat or currach – than it was to walk it or cycle it by road, especially if they had a heavy load to bring home with them. In the old days, boats travelled to Gairfeanach from Leitir Calaidh and other villages and when a sea tragedy occurred in 1905 just south of Inis Treabhair near a very small island known as Geabhóg – the people aboard the boat that sank were actually returning from Tigh Chonraí's and loaded down with provisions when the accident happened. Tragically, five people were drowned and just one person survived – Pádraic na Cataí Ó Conaire from Rosmuc, the father of writer Pádraic Óg Ó Conaire – he managed to grab onto an oar and swam over to Rosmuc with it.

In addition to running a busy shop in Gairfeanach, Michael Chonraí also worked as a travel agent and it was there that people bought their tickets for America, given that there was huge emigration at the time. I remember my uncle coming home from the shop one day with a

101

big colour brochure on Australia saying that we children might be interested in it. I'd never heard of Australia before that and this brochure really stoked my curiosity about this country on the other side of the world. Little did I think then, that I would visit that country myself one day. While Australia is considered a long way from Ireland these days, just imagine how far away that country was from Inis Treabhair in the 1960s!

Back then, I'd heard a good deal more on the news about another faraway country that was over in that part of the world too – i.e. Vietnam. And it was Sonaí Chóilín that was responsible for this too. He was always a great man for the news and was very interested in world affairs and in life generally. And he often spoke about Vietnam and the war that was going on there. He must have been following the story on a daily basis while listening to the radio. He caught the news on the radio every day and if it ever got broken it was over to us that he brought it; we'd bring it into Galway for him then to get fixed. There was a story about Sonaí – whether true or not – that he was changing a battery in the radio one night in such a hurry – in case he missed any bit of the news – that one of the wires inside got twisted and the battery didn't fit properly. He got so annoyed and flustered at the delay so that he cut the loose wire out of the way with a penknife! The poor man had no news for a fortnight afterwards while the radio was being repaired. He read the newspaper regularly also but his eyesight wasn't great in his last years and you often heard him giving out about it – 'Níl mé in ann a léamh ach na *headlines*'/'All I can read are the headlines' he'd say.

To be honest, I don't remember now what 'take' Sonaí Chóilín had on the war in Vietnam – or the 'American War' as the people of Vietnam called it – from what I understand, he was afraid that the Communists and the Russians would take over the world. As for myself, given that I was very small at the time, I probably didn't even understand what the word 'war' meant never mind 'Vietnam'. And yet even if I didn't fully understand the word 'Vietnam', there was still something exotic and mysterious about that foreign name that stayed with me and embedded itself in my mind for a long time afterwards. For years afterwards, I always wanted to put an image to the place that was Vietnam in my mind and see the country in the flesh. And in recent years, I've been lucky enough to visit that country a few times. I've hiked my way across the country and seen many of the killing fields where the horrific carnage of war took place for myself. I've seen some of the battlefields where the rockets and mines tore so many US soldiers apart. I've stood in the giant hollows and pits where the rockets and mines exploded in the earth. I've seen the craters made by the thousands of bombs that fell from the sky on that country and which are still visible in the ground to this day in many areas. I've even crawled my way along through the terrifying tunnels of Cu Chi, of which there are thousands upon thousands of them still buried underground. And I've met some of the people who experienced the dread and horror of a war that has left a permanent scar on so many of the population of Vietnam. It's important to say this too however. I've also been privileged to meet many of the younger generation there, that generation that are creating the new and vibrant Vietnam of today. On top of that, I've had the good fortune to appreciate the extraordinary beauty of the landscape there and the incredible warmth and welcome the Vietnamese people have always been renowned for.

Sonaí Chóilín was quite a religious man even if you often heard him cursing as well! The phrase 'blood an''ouns' (i.e. 'blood and wounds') was on the tip of his tongue regularly, a phrase that you'd rarely hear today. This phrase wasn't one that we had in our house back then either so that, as children, we often found ourselves imitating him just for the fun of it. As with many people of his generation, Sonaí had a belief in various superstitions and there were stories told about him turning home on mornings he was about to go out fishing if a red-haired woman crossed his path.

He came on our trips to Knock with us nearly every

year. My father and mother brought the whole family to Knock shrine once a year in the van. It was always towards the end of summer when the work was all done that we made the journey – once we'd the hay saved and the turf was brought home – just before we went back to school. One of us would be sent over to Sonaí Chóilín's house the evening beforehand to tell him that we were going to Knock the following day. 'Oh,' he'd say, 'I'll have to have a shave and get myself ready.' It was always Sonaí Chóilín who gave out the rosary that we said in the van on the way down. I'm not sure whether it was as part of the pilgrimage itself that we said the rosary or whether it was partly to shorten the road, a journey that took up to two hours at that time. But I do know that it was always an important part of the trip for us to say the holy Rosary on the way to the shrine.

Once Sonaí Chóilín got old and his health began to fail, it really bothered him that he couldn't attend mass every Sunday in Leitir Móir. Apparently, he asked the then parish priest Father Walsh whether it was all right if he listened to the mass on the radio when he couldn't get over as far as the church on the mainland. 'But he told me that this wouldn't do', Sonaí Chóilín used to say. This was the response the priest gave him by all accounts but when he asked his successor, Father Whelan, this same question – when the latter was conducting the stations on the island – he told him that it was fine to listen to mass on the radio if he couldn't make it as far as the church. This, of course, was an era when the majority of people accepted the word of the priest, every priest, as gospel.

At the time, the priest regularly visited people on the island who were unable to attend mass to hear their confession and give them holy communion. 'I'll be visiting the old and the sick,' the priest in Leitir Móir used to say as part of the announcements at the end of mass every Sunday, and he'd list all the villages that he intending visiting and the days of the week he'd call. Neither Inis Treabhair nor Inis Bearachain was ever on the list because of the difficulties associated with getting into the island and the fact that there weren't so many old people living on the islands anyway because the population was so small. The priest would visit them on the day the stations was held however if they were unable to come as far as the station house. And, of course, the priest also called to anoint people who were dying and give them the last rites if it was at all possible.

This was the case with Sonaí Chóilín the night he died. He'd been given the last rites just shortly before this and he was on his deathbed for more than a week so that his death wasn't that unexpected really, as far as I can remember.

I went over to his house with my mother that Sunday night. To tell you the truth I don't remember an awful lot about that night because it's fifty years ago now. I do remember myself and my mother down on our knees in the kitchen saying the rosary and other people back in the room responding to the prayers. We were saying the prayers over and back to one another when Sonaí Chóilín died. I remember going back into the room shortly afterwards and kneeling close to his bed. He hadn't shaved for a while I noticed; and he was wearing a white shirt with blue stripes – one of those shirts that was quite common at the time – over which he wore a heavy, blue woollen jumper. This wasn't unusual of course because they didn't have central heating in most houses at the time, and it was the middle of deepest winter.

Walking home that night, my mother told me that the king of the Island was dead. She said this as Sonaí Chóilín was the oldest person on the island then. It wasn't that we had a tradition on the island to choose or elect a king as happens on Tory Island in Donegal. My father and one of my brothers went to Sonaí Chóilín's house later that night and helped to lay him out. Another neighbour by the name of Peter Dharachín Chátháin went with them and I'm not sure who else. I think that they cut his clothes off him with a scissors initially before washing and shaving him. Sonaí Chóilín had the reputation of being a little bit cranky at times and this was obvious to anyone immediately from the mean, sideways, glance he might give you!

Anyways the story goes that whatever way they turned his head at one stage while they were laying him out or shaving him, didn't he open one of his eyes as much as to say that he was looking askance at Peter Dharachín. Poor Peter got an awful fright for a second thinking that Sonaí was still alive and that he'd come back from the dead!

I remember bottles of whiskey, two barrels of porter, and the like being brought over to his house the next day to wake him. I remember seeing Sonaí laid out, looking all neat and clean-shaven. This was the first time and, indeed, the last time – that I saw someone laid out on the island – and I suppose it made a strong impression on me as a consequence.

A year later, and Christmas on the island would be very different for me than before. I'd be setting out for secondary school in Galway city. This was an aspect of island life that we accepted as the norm from a very young age, as we'd seen older siblings in the family preparing themselves for the same journey and setting out for boarding school. It was neither practical or feasible for us to travel across the bay every day by currach to Eanach Mheáin for school in Scoil Chuimsitheach Chiaráin in An Cheathrú Rua (Carraroe). This had been the same for the majority of teachers who'd taught on Inis Treabhair down through the years. They'd normally travel over on the Monday morning and stay on the island until the

Friday evening. While I lived there, the girls generally went to secondary school in Spiddal or in Oranmore and the boys to Saint Mary's College or Coláiste Éinde (Saint Enda's College) in Galway. All of these schools were boarding schools at the time in addition to catering to for day-pupils.

I went to Coláiste Éinde when I was thirteen years old. I didn't mind heading off to boarding school there. In fact, I was quite happy to get away from the island for a while. As with emigration to America and England, a pattern that was deeply embedded in the people's bones, this temporary 'emigration' or movement to the boarding schools was part and parcel of who we were from a very young age. We'd watched the older brothers and sisters stocking up and packing their bags as the holidays came to an end each year. My mother buying new clothes for them for the next term, and sowing their names onto them, just the same as she did for me when my time came. There was a shop on High Street in Galway city called Tigh Neachtain Beag, as managed by Sonaí Molloy that provided packets of labels or name-tags; these labels comprised very thin strips of white cloth with people's names stitched in red onto them by machine. Michael J. Conneely was on mine and my mother sewed my name onto every item of clothing I owned, from my socks to my jacket.

This was the system which was followed for years. You

brought your own pillows, sheets and blankets with you on starting boarding school and by sewing the names on every item, it limited the chances that anyone might steal clothes from someone else. But the main reason these labels were used was that the pupils sent bags of clothes out to the laundry in the city and in case any of the bags split and the clothes got mixed up. If someone didn't recognise an item of clothing when it came back from the laundry, they could tell from the label who owned what.

But the thing that I liked best was the football boots and the gear we had in secondary school – as we'd never had anything like that on the island. What business would we have had with them? In our final years in Coláiste Éinde, we were let home every three weeks or so but when I first went there, we were only allowed home at Halloween, Christmas and Easter – and maybe on Saint Patrick's Day depending on what day of the week it fell on. I'd been a full two months away from home therefore on returning to Inis Treabhair for the first time in Halloween, 1975 and I remember being taken aback the minute I walked through the door at home again. The house seemed so small and narrow compared to how I remembered it; especially after two months away in an enormous building with hallways so wide that four or five pupils could run a fifty-metre race up and down them – as long as none of the school authorities caught them doing it, that is. This was the same for every pupil from an island on returning from their first stint in boarding school by all accounts. Irish-language writer Breandán Ó hEithir recounted having this same feeling on returning to Inis Mór from his first stint in Coláiste Éinde also: 'How small the house seemed compared to the college' – and I heard the same thing from another islander – the broadcaster Máirtín Jamesie, when he was on the radio one day and recounting his schooldays in the same school.

It wasn't just the house that felt small and restricted now though. My native island Inis Treabhair also felt small too. Incredibly small. Way too small and confined in fact. In truth, I'd never feel really at home there on the island again and I'd always find myself looking out across the sea from then on – over to the mainland, over there to the larger world outside and the new freedom and independence that accompanied it. The opportunity to walk and travel wherever I wanted to travel, and to fly wherever I wanted to fly; the opportunity to explore the wider world beyond the island. From then on, Inis Treabhair always gave me a feeling of confinement or entrapment and there was no way that I would accept such an existence.

APPENDIX

CHRISTMAS POEMS

I was first introduced to Máirtín Ó Direáin's poetry in the national school in Inis Treabhair. I found it easy to relate to and to fall in love with the words, the images, the poetry.

Later I would study his poems for the Leaving cert in St Enda's College in Galway where he once visited our class and read to us when he was writer-in-residence in UCG. I had the honour of introducing him. Later again I would study his work in UCG including his Christmas poems and finally become the publisher of his collected poems.

Máirtín Ó Direáin, 1910–1988 was a fellow islander. Born in Inis Mór, the largest of the Aran islands, he spent most of his life as a civil servant in Dublin where obviously he often thought and wrote about his island home in Aran. He wrote over 400 poems in Irish, several of them about Christmas on the island, looking back and I thought it would be a fitting end to this book to include two of his Christmas poems here. The translations are by the Belfast poet, Frank Sewell.

COINNLE AR LASADH

MÁIRTÍN Ó DIREÁIN

In oileán beag i gcéin san iarthar
Beidh coinnle ar lasadh anocht,
I dtithe ceann tuí, is i dtithe ceann slinne,
Dhá cheann déag de choinnle geala a bheas ar lasadh
anocht.

Mo chaoinbheannacht siar leis na coinnle geala
A bheas ar lasadh anocht,
Is céad beannacht faoi dhó
Le lámh amháin a lasfas coinnle anocht.

(Oíche Chinn an Dá Lá Dhéag, 1939)

CANDLES LIT

In a little island away in the west
There will be candles lit tonight;
In thatched and in slate-roofed housed,
Twelve bright candles lit tonight.

I send a tender blessing west
To the bright candles lit tonight,
And twice a hundred times I bless
One hand lighting candles tonight.

(Twelfth Night of Christmas, 1939)

CUIREADH DO MHUIRE

Nollaig 1942

An eol duit, a Mhuire,
Cá rachair i mbliana
Ag iarraidh foscaidh
Do do Leanbh Naofa,
Tráth a bhfuil gach doras
Dúnta Ina éadan
Ag fuath is uabhar
An chine dhaonna?

Deonaigh glacadh
Le cuireadh uaimse
Go hoileán mara
San iarthar cianda:
Beidh coinnle geala
I ngach fuinneog lasta
Is tine mhóna
Ar theallach adhanta.

AN INVITATION

Christmas 1942

Mary, do you know
Where to go this year
To find some shelter
For your Holy Child
When every door
Is bolted against Him
By the pride and hatred
Of the human race?

Please accept
My invitation
To a seagirt island
Away in the west:
In every window,
Candles will be lit
And in every hearth
A turf fire set.

COLOURFUL IRISH PHRASES

Micheál Ó Conghaile

The Irish language has made a huge contribution to the English language as it's spoken in Ireland and beyond. Micheál Ó Conghaile's *Colourful Irish Phrases* is a small compendium of characteristic phrases that will alert the reader to the unmistakable difference between our native language and English. Even the most basic words are expressed so differently. Please in Irish is *más é do thoil é* (if it is your will), and thanks becomes *go raibh maith agat* (may you receive good). There are many phrases that when translated, word for word, they sound different, unusual and sometimes funny. But above all, they are rich and deeply rooted. Visitors to Ireland who want to get some notion of our native identity will find these phrases both instructive and revealing. Topics covered range across subjects as diverse as insults and put-downs, being human and the gift of the gab.